WILD ABOUT
SPACE

WILD ABOUT
SPACE

WRITTEN BY
SUE BECKLAKE, STEVE PARKER

Little Hippo
Books

First published in 2017 by Miles Kelly Publishing Ltd
Harding's Barn, Bardfield End Green, Thaxted, Essex, CM6 3PX, UK

Copyright © Miles Kelly Publishing Ltd 2017

2 4 6 8 10 9 7 5 3 1

Publishing Director Belinda Gallagher
Creative Director Jo Cowan
Editorial Director Rosie Neave
Senior Editor Fran Bromage
Editorial Assistant Meghan Oosterhuis
Cover Designer Joe Jones
Designers Rob Hale, Joe Jones, Andrea Slane
Image Manager Liberty Newton
Indexer Jane Parker
Production Elizabeth Collins
Reprographics Stephan Davis
Consultants Sue Becklake, Clive Gifford, Steve Parker, Clint Twist

All rights reserved. No part of this publication may be reproduced, stored in a retrieval system, or transmitted by any means, electronic, mechanical, photocopying, recording, or otherwise, without the prior permission of the copyright holder.

ISBN 978-1-960009-32-6

Printed in China

Made with paper from a sustainable forest

littlehippobooks.com

Contents

SPACE	6
Our life-giving star	8
A family of planets	10
Planet of life	12
The Earth's neighbors	14
The smallest of all	16
The biggest of all	18
So far away	20
Comets, asteroids, and meteors	22
A star is born	24
Death of a star	26
Billions of galaxies	28
What is the Universe?	30
Three, two, one... lift-off!	32
Living in space	34
Home from home	36
Robot explorers	38
Watching the Earth	40
Voyage to the Moon	42
Are we alone?	44

ASTRONOMY	46
Families of stars	48
Starry skies	50
Mapping the stars	52
Keeping time	54
Wandering stars	56
First telescopes	58
Discoveries with telescopes	60
How telescopes work	62
Telescopes today	64
Observatories	66
Splitting light	68
Space telescopes	70
Radio telescopes	72
Watching the Sun	74
The edge of the Universe	76
Up close	78
Astronomy from home	80
Past, present, and future	82

EXPLORING SPACE	84
Who explores, and why?	86
Early explorers	88
Man on the Moon	90
Plan and prepare	92
Blast-off!	94
In deep space	96
Ready to explore	98
Flyby, bye-bye	100
Into orbit	102
Landers and impactors	104
Robotic rovers	106
Close-up look	108
Exploring Mars	110
Back on Earth	112
Toward the Sun	114
Asteroids near and far	116
Comet mysteries	118
Gas giants	120

SPACE TRAVEL	122
Escape from Earth	124
Rocket power	126
Space shuttle	128
Returning to Earth	130
Spacecraft	132
Astronauts	134
Space pioneers	136
Spacesuits	138
Spacewalks	140
Living in space	142
Space stations	144
Space tourists	146
Exploring the Moon	148
Satellites at work	150
Long distance space travel	152
Robot travelers	154
A visit to Mars?	156
INDEX	158
ACKNOWLEDGMENTS	160

SPACE

1 Space is all around Earth, high above the air. Here on Earth we are surrounded by air. If you go upward—for example, by climbing a high mountain or flying in a plane—the air grows thinner until there is none at all. Space officially begins 62 miles up from sea level. It is mostly empty, but there are many exciting things such as planets, stars, and galaxies. People who travel in space are called astronauts.

▶ In space, astronauts wear spacesuits to go outside a space station or a spacecraft as it circles Earth. Much farther away are planets, stars, and galaxies.

Our life-giving star

2 **The Sun is our nearest star.** Most stars are so far away they look like points of light in the sky, but the Sun looks different because it is much closer to us. The Sun is not solid, like Earth. It is a huge ball of super-hot gases, so hot that they glow like the flames of a bonfire.

◀ The Sun's hot, glowing gas is always on the move, bubbling up to the surface and sinking back down again.

3 **Nothing could live on Earth without the Sun.** Deep in its center the Sun is constantly making energy that keeps its gases hot and glowing. This energy works its way to the surface where it escapes as heat and light. Without it, Earth would be cold and dark with no life at all.

PROMINENCE

Solar prominences can reach temperatures of 18,000°F.

SOLAR FLARE

Solar flares erupt in a few minutes, then take more than half an hour to die away again.

SUNSPOT
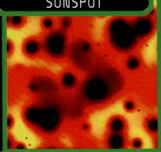
Groups of sunspots seem to move across the Sun over two weeks, as the Sun rotates.

SPACE

4 **The Sun is often spotty.** Sunspots appear on the surface, some wider than Earth. They look dark because they are cooler than the rest of the Sun. Solar flares—explosions of energy—can suddenly shoot out from the Sun. The Sun also throws huge loops of gas called prominences out into space.

▶ When the Moon casts a shadow on Earth, there is a solar eclipse.

5 **When the Moon hides the Sun there is a solar eclipse.** Every so often, the Sun, Moon, and Earth line up in space so that the Moon comes directly between the Earth and the Sun. This stops the sunlight from reaching a small area on Earth. This area grows dark and cold, as if night has come early.

▲ A photo of a solar eclipse on August 1, 2008 shows the Moon totally blocking the Sun, and reveals the Sun's halolike corona—part of its atmosphere not normally seen because the Sun's surface is too bright.

I DON'T BELIEVE IT!
The surface of the Sun is nearly 60 times hotter than boiling water. It is so hot it would melt a spacecraft flying near it.

WARNING
Never look directly at the Sun, especially not through a telescope or binoculars. It is so bright it will harm your eyes and could even make you blind.

A family of planets

6 The Sun is surrounded by a family of circling planets called the Solar System. This family is held together by an invisible force called gravity, which pulls things toward each other. It is the same force that pulls us down to the ground and stops us from floating away. The Sun's gravity pulls on the planets and keeps them circling around it.

I DON'T BELIEVE IT!
If the Sun was the size of a large beach ball, Earth would be as small as a pea, and the Moon would look like a pinhead.

7 Earth is one of eight planets in the Sun's family. They all circle the Sun at different distances from it. The four planets nearest to the Sun are all balls of rock. The other four planets are much bigger and are made of gas and liquid.

SPACE

▼ The eight planets are all different. Mercury, nearest the Sun, is small and hot. Then Venus, Earth, and Mars are rocky and cooler. Beyond them Jupiter, Saturn, Uranus, and Neptune are large and cold.

8 **Moons circle the planets, traveling with them round the Sun.** Earth has one moon. It circles Earth while Earth circles round the Sun. Mars has two tiny moons, but Mercury and Venus have none at all. There are large families of moons, like miniature solar systems, around all the large gas planets.

9 **There are millions of smaller members in the Sun's family.** Some are tiny specks of dust speeding through space between the planets. Larger chunks of rock, many as large as mountains, are called asteroids. Comets come from the edge of the Solar System, skimming past the Sun before they disappear again.

Planet of life

Location of Earth

10 **The planet we live on is called Earth.** It is a round ball of rock. On the outside (where we live) the rock is hard and solid. But deep below our feet, inside the Earth, the rock is hot enough to melt. You can sometimes see this hot rock showering out of an erupting volcano.

Inner core
Outer core
Mantle
Crust
Atmosphere

▶ Earth's inner core is made of iron. It is very hot and keeps the outer core as liquid. Outside this is the mantle, made of thick rock. The thin surface layer that we live on is called the crust.

▼ No other planet in the Solar System has liquid water on its surface, so Earth is the only known planet suitable for life.

11 **Earth is the only planet with life.** From space, Earth is a blue-and-white planet, with huge oceans and wet masses of cloud. Animals—including people—and plants can live on Earth because of all this water.

12 **Sunshine gives us daylight when it is night on the other side of the Earth.** When it is daytime, your part of the Earth faces toward the Sun and it is light. At night, your part faces away from the Sun and it is dark. Day follows night because the Earth is always turning.

As Earth rotates, the day and night halves shift gradually around the world. Earth turns eastward, so the Sun rises in the east as each part of the world spins to face it.

I DON'T BELIEVE IT!
The Moon has no air. When astronauts went to the Moon they had to take air with them in their spacecraft and spacesuits.

13 **Craters on the Moon are scars from space rocks crashing into the surface.** When a rock smashes into the Moon at high speed, it leaves a saucer-shaped dent, pushing some of the rock outward into a ring of mountains.

14 **Look for the Moon on clear nights and watch how it seems to change shape.** Over a month it changes from a thin crescent to a round shape. This is because sunlight is reflected by the Moon. We see the full Moon when the side that faces Earth is lit by the Sun, and a thin crescent shape when most of the far side is lit.

Crescent moon

Half moon

Full moon

Half moon

Crescent moon

▲ During the first half of each monthly cycle, the Moon waxes (appears to grow). During the second half, it wanes (dwindles) back to a crescent-shape.

▲ Dark patches are called seas although there is no water on the Moon.

The Earth's neighbors

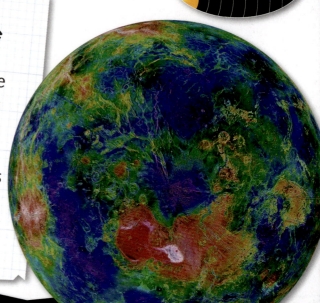

Location of Venus

15 **Venus and Mars are the nearest planets to Earth.** Venus is closer to the Sun than Earth while Mars is farther away. Each takes a different amount of time to circle the Sun and we call this its year. A year on Venus is 225 days, on Earth 365 days, and on Mars 687 days.

16 **Venus is the hottest planet, even though Mercury is closer to the Sun.** Heat builds up on Venus because it is completely covered by clouds that trap the heat, like the glass in a greenhouse.

▲ Dense clouds surround Venus, making it difficult to observe, so the *Magellan* spacecraft spent four years mapping the surface with radar (bouncing radio waves) to produce images like this.

▲ Under its clouds, Venus has hundreds of volcanoes, large and small, all over its surface. We do not know if any of them are still erupting.

17 **The clouds around Venus are poisonous—they contain drops of acid that would burn your skin.** They are not like clouds on Earth, which are made of droplets of water. They are thick, and do not let much sunshine reach the surface of Venus.

SPACE

Location of Mars

18 **Winds on Mars whip up huge dust storms that can cover the whole planet.** Mars is very dry, like a desert, and covered in red dust. When a space probe called *Mariner 9* arrived there in 1971, the whole planet was hidden by dust clouds.

▲ *Mariner 9* was the first space probe to circle another planet. Since that time more than 30 other crafts have traveled to Mars and several have soft-landed including six rovers.

Solar panel — Camera — Radio aerial

19 **Mars has the largest volcano in the Solar System.** It is called Olympus Mons and is three times as high as Mount Everest, the tallest mountain on Earth. Olympus Mons is an old volcano and it has not erupted for millions of years.

LIFE ON MARS
Mars is the best known planet besides Earth. It is dry, rocky, and covered in dust. Look in books and on the Internet to find out more about Mars. What do you think it would be like to live there?

20 **There are plans to send astronauts to Mars but the journey would take six months or more.** The astronauts would have to take with them everything they need for the journey there and back and for their stay on Mars.

◀ The Hubble Space Telescope has captured a giant dust storm in this picture of Mars. The bright orange patch in the middle shows where the dry red dust is blown up by strong winds.

The smallest of all

Location of Mercury

21 **Mercury looks like our Moon.** It is a round, cratered ball of rock. Although a little larger than the Moon, like the Moon it has no air.

MAKE CRATERS
You will need:
flour   baking sheet
a marble or a stone

1. Spread some flour about an inch deep on a baking sheet and smooth over the surface.
2. Drop a marble or a small round stone onto the flour.
3. Can you see the saucer-shaped crater the marble makes?

◀ Mercury has high cliffs and long ridges as well as craters. Astronomers think it cooled and shrank in the past, making its surface wrinkled.

CRATERS

Mercury's many craters show how often it was hit by space rocks. One was so large that it shattered rocks on the other side of the planet.

22 **The sunny side of Mercury is boiling hot but the night side is freezing cold.** Being the nearest planet to the Sun, the sunny side can get twice as hot as an oven. But Mercury spins round slowly so the night side has time to cool down, and there is no air to trap the heat. The night side becomes more than twice as cold as Antarctica—the coldest place on Earth.

SPACE

Location of dwarf planets

23 Tiny, rocky Pluto was discovered in 1930. At first it was called a planet, but in 2006, it was reclassified as a dwarf planet. It is less than half the width of Mercury. In fact, Pluto is smaller than our Moon.

25 Aside from Pluto, four other dwarf planets have been named in our solar system. They are called Ceres, Eris, Makemake, and Haumea.

ERIS

PLUTO

CERES

▲ Ceres orbits between Mars and Jupiter. Pluto orbits further away from the Sun than Neptune, and Eris is further out still. This artists' impression is not to scale.

24 If you stood on the surface of Pluto, the Sun would not look much brighter than any other stars. Pluto is so far from the Sun that it receives little heat and is completely covered in ice.

26 *New Horizons* is the first space probe to visit Pluto. It blasted off in 2006 and reached the dwarf planet in July 2015. It is now exploring the outer region of the Solar System, called the Kuiper Belt.

The biggest of all

Location of Jupiter

27 Jupiter is more massive than the other seven planets in the Solar System put together. It is 11 times as wide as Earth, although it is still much smaller than the Sun. Saturn, the next largest planet, is more than nine times as wide as the Earth.

28 Jupiter has more than 70 moons. Its moon Io has many active volcanoes that throw out huge plumes of material, making red blotches and dark marks on its orange-yellow surface.

29 The Great Red Spot on Jupiter is a 300-year-old storm. It was first noticed about 300 years ago and is at least twice as wide as the Earth. It rises above the rest of the clouds and swirls around like storm clouds on Earth.

◀ Jupiter's fast winds blow clouds into colored bands around the planet.

▼ There are many storms on Jupiter but none are as large or long-lasting as the Great Red Spot.

These four large moons were discovered by Galileo Galilei in 1610, which is why they are known as the Galilean moons.

SPACE

Location of Saturn

▶ Although Saturn's rings are very wide, they stretch out in a very thin layer around the planet.

30 The shining rings around Saturn are made of millions of chunks of ice. These circle the planet like tiny moons and shine by reflecting sunlight from their surfaces. Some are as small as ice cubes while others are as large as a car.

31 Jupiter and Saturn are gas giants. They have no solid surface for a spacecraft to land on. All that you can see are the tops of their clouds. Beneath the clouds, the planets are made mostly of gas (like air) and liquid (water is a liquid).

▼ Taken with the Hubble Space Telescope, this image shows a detailed view of Saturn's southern hemisphere and its rings.

I DON'T BELIEVE IT!
For its size, Saturn is lighter than any other planet. If there was a large enough sea, it would float like a cork.

32 Jupiter and Saturn spin around so fast that they bulge out in the middle. This can happen because they are not made of solid rock. As they spin, their clouds are stretched out into light and dark bands around them.

So far away

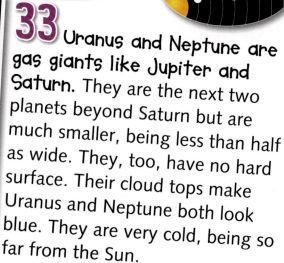

▲ This photo shows an aurora display (the glowing blue dot) on Uranus. Aurorae are made by tiny particles given off by the Sun, known as the solar wind. These get trapped by a planet's magnetism and start to glow.

33 Uranus and Neptune are gas giants like Jupiter and Saturn. They are the next two planets beyond Saturn but are much smaller, being less than half as wide. They, too, have no hard surface. Their cloud tops make Uranus and Neptune both look blue. They are very cold, being so far from the Sun.

▶ Uranus's moon Miranda looks as though it has been split apart and put back together again.

34 Uranus seems to "roll" around the Sun. Most of the other planets spin upright like tops, but Uranus spins on its side. It may have been knocked over when something crashed into it millions of years ago.

▼ Uranus's five largest moons are big enough to be classified as dwarf planets, but they are not in direct orbit of the Sun.

	Name	Diameter	Year of discovery
1	Titania	980 miles	1787
2	Oberon	946 miles	1787
3	Umbriel	726 miles	1851
4	Ariel	720 miles	1851
5	Miranda	293 miles	1948

35 Uranus has more than 25 moons, and there are probably more to be discovered. Most are very small, but Titania, the largest, is 980 miles across, which makes it the eighth largest moon in the Solar System.

SPACE

Location of Neptune

36 **Neptune had a storm that disappeared.** When the *Voyager 2* space probe flew past Neptune in 1989 it spotted a huge storm, like a dark version of the Great Red Spot on Jupiter. But when the Hubble Space Telescope looked at Neptune in 1994, the storm had gone.

QUIZ

1. How many moons does Uranus have?
2. When was Uranus's moon Miranda discovered?
3. Which planet seems to "roll" around the Sun?
4. What color are Neptune's clouds?

Answers:
1. More than 25 2. 1948 3. Uranus 4. Blue

▲ *Voyager 2* is the only probe to visit Neptune and send back close up pictures of the planet.

37 **Neptune has bright blue clouds that make the whole planet look blue.** Above them are smaller white streaks—icy clouds that race around the planet. One of these clouds, seen by the *Voyager 2* space probe, was named "Scooter" because it scooted around the planet so fast.

38 **Neptune is sometimes farther from the Sun than Pluto.** Planets and dwarf planets go around the Sun on orbits (paths) that look like circles, but Pluto's path is more squashed. This sometimes brings it closer to the Sun than Neptune.

Sun — Neptune — Pluto
Orbit of Pluto
Orbit of Neptune

▲ Neptune is so far from the Sun that its orbit lasts 164.79 Earth years. It has only completed one orbit since it was discovered in 1846.

Comets, asteroids, and meteors

39 There are probably billions of tiny comets at the edge of the Solar System. They circle the Sun far beyond Neptune. Sometimes one is disturbed and moves inward toward the Sun, looping around it before going back to where it came from. Some comets come back to the Sun regularly—Halley's comet returns every 76 years.

The solid part of a comet is hidden inside a huge, glowing cloud that stretches into a long tail.

40 A comet is often called a dirty snowball because it is made of dust and ice mixed together. Heat from the Sun melts some of the ice. This makes dust and gas stream away from the comet, forming a huge tail that glows in the sunlight.

41 Comet tails always point away from the Sun. Although it looks bright, a comet's tail is extremely thin so it is blown outward, away from the Sun.

SPACE

42 **Asteroids are chunks of rock that failed to stick together to make a planet.** Most of them circle the Sun between Mars and Jupiter where there would be room for another planet. There are millions of asteroids, some the size of a car, and others as big as mountains.

ASTEROIDS

43 **Meteors are sometimes called shooting stars.** They are not really stars, just streaks of light that flash across the night sky. Meteors are made when pebbles racing through space at high speed hit the top of the air above the Earth. The pebble gets so hot it burns up. We see it as a glowing streak for a few seconds.

Asteroids travel in a ring around the Sun. This ring is called the asteroid belt and can be found between Mars and Jupiter.

▼ This crater in Arizona is one of the few large meteorite (a meteor that hits Earth) craters visible on Earth. The Moon is covered in them.

QUIZ

1. Which way does a comet tail always point?
2. What is another name for a meteor?
3. Where is the asteroid belt?

Answers:
1. Away from the Sun 2. Shooting star 3. Between Mars and Jupiter

A star is born

44 **Stars are born in clouds of dust and gas called nebulae.** Astronomers can see these clouds as shining patches in the night sky, or dark patches against the distant stars. These clouds shrink as gravity pulls the dust and gas together. At the center, the gas gets hotter and hotter until a new star is born.

45 **Stars begin their lives when they start making energy.** When the dust and gas pulls tightly together it gets very hot. Finally it gets so hot in the middle that it can start making energy. The energy makes the star shine, giving out heat and light like the Sun.

QUIZ

1. What is a nebula?
2. How long has the Sun been shining?
3. What color are large hot stars?
4. What is a group of new young stars called?

Answers:
1. A cloud of dust and gas in space 2. About 4.6 billion years 3. Bluish-white 4. Star cluster

KEY

❶ Clumps of gas in a nebula start to shrink into the tight round balls that will become stars. The gas spirals around as it is pulled inward.

❷ Deep in its center, the new star starts making energy, but it is still hidden by the cloud of dust and gas.

❸ The dust and gas are blown away and we can see the star shining. Any left over gas and dust may form planets around the new star.

SPACE

STAR CLUSTER

46 Young stars often stay together in clusters. When they start to shine they light up the nebula, making it glow with bright colors. Then the starlight blows away the remains of the cloud and we can see a group of new stars, called a star cluster.

This cluster of young stars, with many stars of different colors and sizes, will gradually drift apart, breaking up the cluster.

47 Large stars are very hot and white, smaller stars are cooler and redder. A large star can make energy faster and get much hotter than a smaller star. This gives them a very bright, bluish-white color. Smaller stars are cooler. This makes them look red and shine less brightly. Ordinary in-between stars—like our Sun—look yellow.

48 Smaller stars live much longer than huge stars. Stars use up their gas to make energy, and the largest stars use up their gas much faster than smaller stars. The Sun is about halfway through its life. It has been shining for about 4.6 billion years and will go on shining for another 5 billion years.

25

Death of a star

RED GIANT STAR

49 Stars begin to die when they run out of gas to make energy. The middle of the star begins to shrink but the outer parts expand, making the star much larger.

At the end of their lives stars swell up into red giant stars, as shown in this far infrared image, or even larger red supergiants.

50 Red giant stars are dying stars that have swollen to hundreds of times their normal size. Their expanding outer layers get cooler, making them look red. When the Sun is a red giant it will be large enough to swallow up the nearest planets, Mercury and Venus, and perhaps Earth.

51 Eventually, a red giant's outer layers drift away, making a halo of gas around the star. The starlight makes this gas glow and we call it a planetary nebula. All that is left is a small, hot star called a white dwarf, which cannot make energy and gradually cools and dies.

PLANETARY NEBULA

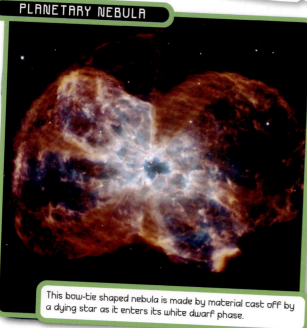

This bow-tie shaped nebula is made by material cast off by a dying star as it enters its white dwarf phase.

WHITE DWARF STARS

These ancient white dwarf stars are in our Milky Way Galaxy, and are between 12 and 13 billion years old.

SPACE

52 **Very heavy stars end their lives in a huge explosion called a supernova.** This explosion blows away all the outer parts of the star. All that is left is a tiny hot star in the middle of a shell of hot glowing gas.

▶ Cassiopeia A is one of the best-studied supernova remnants. This image was made using data from three different types of telescopes.

I DON'T BELIEVE IT!
One of the main signs of a black hole is radiation from very hot gases near one just before they are sucked in.

53 **After a supernova explosion the largest stars may end up as black holes.** The remains of the star fall in on itself. As it shrinks, its gravity gets stronger. Eventually the pull of its gravity can get so strong that nothing near it can escape. This is called a black hole.

▲ Hot gas falling into a black hole called Cygnus X-1 gives out powerful X-rays picked up by the Chandra satellite.

Billions of galaxies

54 The Sun is part of a huge family of stars called the Milky Way Galaxy. There are billions of other stars in our galaxy, as many as the grains of sand on a beach. We call it the Milky Way because it looks like a faint band of light in the night sky, as though someone has spilled some milk across space.

▶ With binoculars you can see that the faint glow of the Milky Way comes from millions of stars in our galaxy.

55 Curling arms give some galaxies their spiral shape. The Milky Way has arms made of bright stars and glowing clouds of gas that curl round into a spiral shape. Some galaxies, called elliptical galaxies, have a round shape like a squashed ball. Other galaxies have no particular shape.

I DON'T BELIEVE IT!
If you could fit the Milky Way onto these two pages, the Sun would be so tiny, you could not see it.

SPACE

A CLUSTER OF GALAXIES

56 There are billions of galaxies outside the Milky Way. Some are larger than the Milky Way and many are smaller, but they all have more stars than you can count. The galaxies tend to stay together in groups called clusters.

Astronomers have nicknamed this interesting cluster of galaxies the "Bullet Cluster." It is made up of two colliding groups of galaxies.

ELLIPTICAL

SPIRAL

IRREGULAR

▲ Galaxies can be categorized by their shape. The Milky Way is a spiral galaxy.

57 There is no bump when galaxies collide. A galaxy is mostly empty space between the stars. But when galaxies get very close they can pull each other out of shape. Sometimes they look as if they have grown a huge tail stretching out into space, or their shape may change into a ring of glowing stars.

▲ These two galaxies are so close that each has pulled a long tail of bright stars from the other.

29

What is the Universe?

58 The Universe is the name we give to everything we know about. This means everything on Earth, from tiny bits of dust to the highest mountain, and everything that lives here. It also means everything in space—all the billions of stars in the billions of galaxies.

59 **The Universe started with a massive explosion called the Big Bang.** Astronomers think that this happened about 13.7 billion years ago. The explosion sent everything racing outward in all directions. To start with, everything was packed incredibly close together. Over time it has expanded (spread out) into the Universe we can see today, which is mostly empty space.

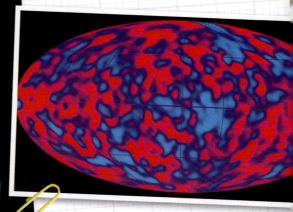

▲ A satellite has measured and mapped the oldest light in the Universe, known as the cosmic microwave background, providing a snapshot of the early Universe.

60 **The Universe's matter includes planets, stars, and gas, and its energy includes light and heat.** Scientists suspect that it also contains unknown dark matter and dark energy, which we are unable to detect. These may affect what finally happens to the Universe.

DARK MATTER

Some of the distant galaxies in this cluster appear distorted, because light coming from them is being bent by invisible dark matter.

SPACE

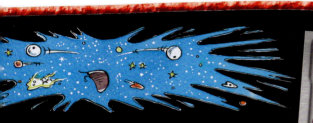

61 **The galaxies are still racing away from each other.** When astronomers look at distant galaxies they can see that other galaxies are moving away from our galaxy, and the more distant galaxies are moving away faster. In fact all the galaxies are moving apart from each other. We say that the Universe is expanding.

DOTTY UNIVERSE
You will need:
balloon   pen

Blow up a balloon a little, holding the neck to stop air escaping. Mark dots on the balloon with a pen, then blow it up some more. Watch how the dots move apart from each other. This is like the galaxies moving apart as the Universe expands.

62 **We do not know what will happen to the Universe billions of years in the future.** It may keep on expanding. If this happens, old stars will gradually die and no new ones will be born. Everywhere will become dark and cold.

KEY

❶ All the parts that make up the Universe were once packed tightly together. No one knows why the Universe started expanding with a Big Bang.

❷ As everything moved apart in all directions, stars and galaxies started to form.

❸ Today there are galaxies of different shapes and sizes, all moving apart. One day they may start moving toward each other.

❹ The Universe could stop expanding, or shrink and end with a Big Crunch.

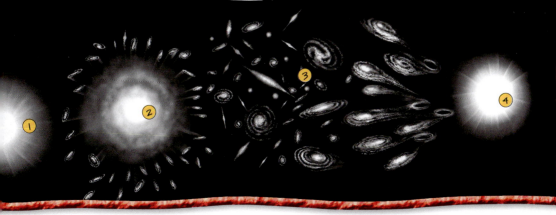

Three, two, one... lift-off!

63 A rocket must travel nearly 40 times faster than a jumbo jet to blast into space. Slower than that, and gravity will pull it back to Earth. Rockets are powered by burning fuel, which makes hot gases. These gases rush out of the engines, shooting the rocket upward.

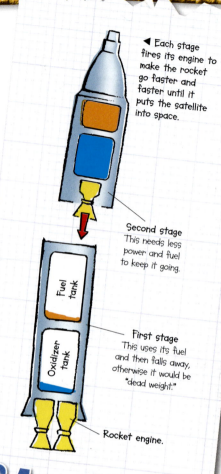

◄ Each stage fires its engine to make the rocket go faster and faster until it puts the satellite into space.

Second stage This needs less power and fuel to keep it going.

Fuel tank

First stage This uses its fuel and then falls away, otherwise it would be "dead weight."

Oxidizer tank

Rocket engine.

This shuttle was blasted into space by three rocket engines and two huge booster rockets.

64 A single rocket is usually not powerful enough to launch a satellite or spacecraft. So most have two or three stages, which are really separate rockets mounted on top of each other, each with its own engines. When the first stage has used up its fuel it drops away, and the second stage starts. Finally the third stage takes over to go into space.

SPACE

65 **Some launchers have boosters.** These are extra rockets fixed to the main one. Most boosters burn solid fuel, like giant firework rockets. They fall away when the fuel has burned up. Some drift down on parachutes into the sea, to be used again.

QUIZ

1. Why did shuttles use parachutes—to stop or to start?
2. How many times faster than a jet does a rocket have to travel to blast into space?
3. What year was the final shuttle mission?

Answers:
1. To stop 2. Forty times faster 3. 2011

The shuttle puts down its wheels and lands on the runway. A parachute and speed brakes bring the shuttle to a standstill.

◀ On July 8, 2011, space shuttle *Atlantis* took off from Florida on the final mission of the 30-year space shuttle program.

66 **The space shuttles were reusable spaceplanes.** The first was launched in 1981 and there were more than 130 missions. The shuttle took off straight up like a rocket, carrying a load of up to 26 tons. To land it swooped down to glide onto a runway.

Living in space

67 **Space is a dangerous place for astronauts.** It can be boiling hot in the sunshine or freezing cold in the Earth's shadow. There is also dangerous radiation from the Sun. Dust, rocks, and bits from other rockets race through space at such speed, they could easily make a small hole in a spacecraft, letting the air leak out.

SPACE WALK

It is not easy for an astronaut wearing a bulky spacesuit to hold tools or bend his or her arms.

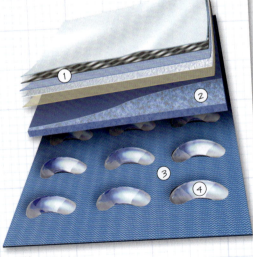

▼ In a spacesuit, many layers of different materials are needed to keep the astronaut safe.

KEY
1. Outer layers protect the wearer from the fierce heat of the Sun.
2. This layer seals the suit from the vacuum of space.
3. Soft lining goes next to the skin.
4. Tubes carrying cooling water.

68 **Spacesuits protect astronauts when they are out in space.** They are very bulky because they are made of many layers to make them strong. They must hold the air for astronauts to breathe and protect them against speeding dust and harmful radiation. To keep the astronauts cool while they work outside the spacecraft, tubes of water under the spacesuit carry away heat.

SPACE

SPACE MEALS

You will need:
dried noodles   boiling water

Buy a dried snack such as noodles. With help from an adult, add boiling water. This is the kind of food astronauts eat. Most of their meals are dried so they are not too heavy to launch into space.

70 Everything floats around in space as if it has no weight. So all objects have to be fixed down or they will float away. Astronauts have footholds to keep them still while they are working. They strap themselves into sleeping bags so they don't bump into things when they are asleep.

69 Astronauts must take everything they need into space with them. Out in space there is no air, water, or food, so all the things that astronauts need to live must be packed into their spacecraft and taken with them.

▶ Sleeping bags are fixed to walls so astronauts look as though they are asleep standing up.

Home from home

71 **A space station is a home in space for astronauts and cosmonauts (Russian astronauts).** It has a kitchen for making meals, and cabins with sleeping bags. There are toilets, wash basins, and sometimes showers. There are places to work, and controls where astronauts can check that everything is working properly.

▼ The International Space Station provides astronauts with a home in space.

72 **Many countries helped to build the International Space Station (ISS) in space.** These include the U.S., Russia, Japan, Canada, Brazil, and European countries. It is built up from separate sections called modules that have been made to fit together like a jigsaw.

73 **The U.S. space station Skylab, launched in 1973, fell back to Earth in 1979.** Most of it landed in the ocean but some pieces hit Australia.

KEY
1. Solar panels for power
2. Space shuttle
3. Docking port
4. Control module
5. Living module
6. Soyuz ferry

SPACE

INTERNATIONAL SPACE STATION

74 Each part was launched from Earth and added to the ISS in space. There they were fitted by astronauts at the ISS with the help of a robot arm. Huge panels of solar cells have been added. These turn sunlight into electricity to provide a power supply for the space station.

An aerial view of a hurricane swirling on Earth is captured by an ISS crew member in September 2010.

75 The crew live on board the ISS for several months at a time. The first crew of three people arrived at the space station in November 2000 and stayed for over four months. The station now has sleeping quarters for six astronauts, and many modules for living and working.

76 People and supplies can travel to the ISS in Russian Soyuz and American Dragon spacecraft. There are also uncrewed cargo vehicles, including Russian Progress spacecraft. In 2001, American Dennis Tito became the first space tourist, staying on the ISS for eight days.

Robot explorers

77 Robot spacecraft called probes have explored all the planets. Probes take close-up pictures and measurements, and send the data back to scientists on Earth. Some probes circle planets taking pictures. For a really close-up look, a probe can land on the surface.

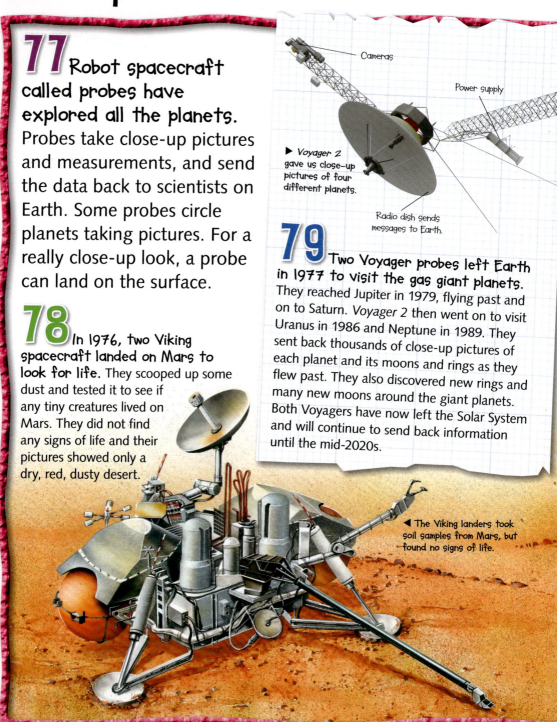

▶ Voyager 2 gave us close-up pictures of four different planets.

Cameras
Power supply
Radio dish sends messages to Earth.

78 In 1976, two Viking spacecraft landed on Mars to look for life. They scooped up some dust and tested it to see if any tiny creatures lived on Mars. They did not find any signs of life and their pictures showed only a dry, red, dusty desert.

79 Two Voyager probes left Earth in 1977 to visit the gas giant planets. They reached Jupiter in 1979, flying past and on to Saturn. Voyager 2 then went on to visit Uranus in 1986 and Neptune in 1989. They sent back thousands of close-up pictures of each planet and its moons and rings as they flew past. They also discovered new rings and many new moons around the giant planets. Both Voyagers have now left the Solar System and will continue to send back information until the mid-2020s.

◀ The Viking landers took soil samples from Mars, but found no signs of life.

SPACE

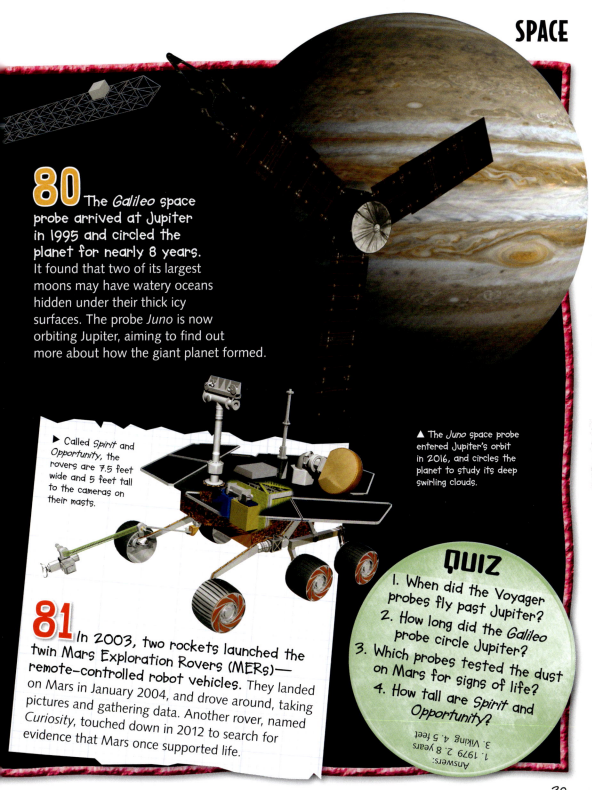

80 The *Galileo* space probe arrived at Jupiter in 1995 and circled the planet for nearly 8 years. It found that two of its largest moons may have watery oceans hidden under their thick icy surfaces. The probe *Juno* is now orbiting Jupiter, aiming to find out more about how the giant planet formed.

▲ The *Juno* space probe entered Jupiter's orbit in 2016, and circles the planet to study its deep swirling clouds.

▶ Called *Spirit* and *Opportunity*, the rovers are 7.5 feet wide and 5 feet tall to the cameras on their masts.

81 In 2003, two rockets launched the twin Mars Exploration Rovers (MERs)—remote-controlled robot vehicles. They landed on Mars in January 2004, and drove around, taking pictures and gathering data. Another rover, named *Curiosity*, touched down in 2012 to search for evidence that Mars once supported life.

QUIZ

1. When did the Voyager probes fly past Jupiter?
2. How long did the *Galileo* probe circle Jupiter?
3. Which probes tested the dust on Mars for signs of life?
4. How tall are *Spirit* and *Opportunity*?

Answers:
1. 1979 2. 8 years 3. Viking 4. 5 feet

Watching the Earth

82 **Hundreds of satellites circle the Earth in space.** They are launched into space by rockets and may stay there for ten years or more.

▼ Weather satellites look down at the clouds and give warning when a violent storm is approaching.

83 **Weather satellites help the forecasters tell us what the weather will be like.** These satellites can see where the clouds are forming and which way they are going. They watch the winds and rain and measure how hot the air and the ground are.

▶ The different satellites each have their own job to do, looking at the Earth, or the weather, or out into space.

84 **Communications satellites carry TV programs and telephone messages around the world.** Large aerials on Earth beam radio signals up to a space satellite that then beams them down to another aerial, half way around the world. This lets us talk to people on the other side of the world, and watch events such as the Olympic Games while they are happening in faraway countries.

▼ Communications satellites can beam TV programs directly to your home through your own aerial dish.

SPACE

85 **Spy satellites circling the Earth take pictures of secret sites around the world.** They can listen to secret radio messages from military ships or aircraft.

▶ Satellite telescopes let astronomers look far out into the Universe and discover what is out there.

▼ Pictures of the Earth taken by satellites can help make very accurate maps.

86 **Earth-watching satellites look out for pollution.** Oil slicks in the sea and dirty air over cities show up clearly in pictures from these satellites. They can help farmers by showing how well crops are growing and by looking for pests and diseases. Spotting forest fires and icebergs that may be a danger to ships is also easier from space.

87 **Satellite telescopes let astronomers look at exciting things in space.** They can see other kinds of radiation, such as X-rays, as well as light. X-ray telescopes can tell astronomers where there may be a black hole.

Voyage to the Moon

88 The first men landed on the Moon in 1969. They were two astronauts from the U.S. *Apollo 11* mission. Neil Armstrong was the first person to set foot on the Moon. There were five other Apollo missions that landed on the moon.

▲ In 1969, about half a billion people watched US astronaut Neil Armstrong's first steps onto another world.

89 The giant *Saturn V* rocket launched the astronauts on their journey to the Moon. It was the largest rocket to have ever been built. Its three stages lifted the astronauts into space, and the third stage gave it an extra boost to send it to the Moon.

Thrusters.

Legs folded for journey.

Lunar Module.

Command Module.

Main engine.

Service Module with fuel and air supplies.

90 The Command Module that carried the astronauts to the Moon had no more room than a station wagon. The astronauts were squashed inside it for the journey, which took three days to get there and another three to get back. On their return, the Command Module, with the astronauts inside, splashed down in the sea.

▲ The Lunar and Command Modules traveled to the Moon fixed together, then separated for the Moon landing.

SPACE

▼ *Apollo 15*, launched in 1971, was the fourth human landing. Here, astronaut Jim Irwin loads the Lunar Rover (right). The Lunar Module is on the left.

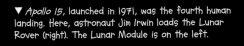

91 **The Lunar Module took two of the astronauts—Neil Armstrong and Edwin "Buzz" Aldrin—to the Moon's surface.** Once safely landed, they put on spacesuits and went outside to collect rocks. Later they took off in the Lunar Module to join the third astronaut—Michael Collins—who had stayed in the Command Module, circling above the Moon on his own.

92 **The Lunar Rover was a moon car for the astronauts to ride on.** It looked like a buggy with four wheels and two seats. It could only travel about as fast as you can run. The astronauts drove for up to 12 miles at a time, exploring the Moon's rocky surface near their landing site.

93 **No one has been back to the Moon since the last Apollo mission left in 1972.** There are plans for people to return in the future, and build bases where they can live and work.

94 **On the way to the Moon in 1970, an explosion damaged the *Apollo 13* spacecraft.** This left the astronauts with little heat or light, but they managed to return safely to Earth.

Are we alone?

95 The only life we have found so far in the Universe is here on Earth. Everywhere you look on Earth from the frozen Antarctic to the hottest, driest deserts, on land and in the sea, there are living things. Some are huge, such as whales and elephants, and others are much too small to see. But they all need water to live.

▼ On Earth, animals can live in a wide range of different habitats, such as in the sea, in deserts and jungles, and icy lands.

DESERT

SEA

POLAR LANDS

RAIN FOREST

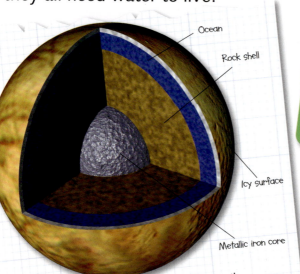

▲ Deep beneath Europa's cracked, icy surface, it may be warm enough for the ice to melt into water.

96 There may be an underground ocean on Europa, one of Jupiter's moons. Europa is a little smaller than our Moon and is covered in ice. However, astronomers think that there may be an ocean of water under the ice. If so, there could be strange living creatures swimming around deep underground.

SPACE

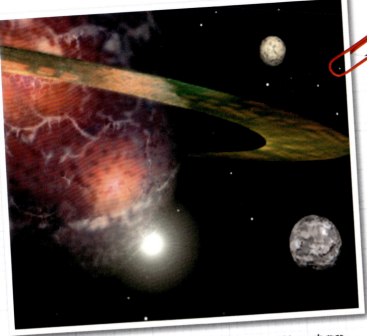

▲ No one knows what other exoplanets would be like. They could have strange moons or colorful rings. Anything that lives there might look very strange to us.

97 Astronomers have found planets circling other stars, called exoplanets. Most of them are large, like Jupiter. But perhaps some could be smaller, like Earth. They could have a rocky surface that is not too hot or too cold, and suitable for liquid water—known as "Goldilocks planets" after the fairytale character who tried the three bears' porridge. These planets could support some kind of life.

98 Mars seems to have had rivers and seas billions of years ago. Astronomers can see dry riverbeds and ridges that look like ocean shores on its surface. This makes them think Mars may have been warm and wet long ago and something may once have lived there. Now it is very cold and dry with no sign of life.

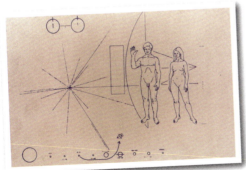

▲ Maybe the Pioneer plaques will be found by aliens who perhaps can read them and come to visit us!

99 Our nearest neighboring star is Proxima Centauri. This star is 4.2 light years away from Earth, which means it would take many thousands of years to reach it using today's spacecraft. Perhaps in the future scientists will discover how we can travel faster than the speed of light!

100 Each Pioneer probe carries a plaque about 9 inches wide. They show pictures of a man and woman, with the Solar System along the bottom and a chart of where the Earth is among the stars. In space the Pioneers will keep going forever, unless they hit something like a moon, a planet, or an asteroid.

ASTRONOMY

101 Astronomy is the study of everything you can see in the night sky and many other things out in space. Astronomers try to find out all about stars and galaxies. They look for planets circling around stars, and at mysterious explosions far out in space. Telescopes help them to see further, spotting things that are much too faint to see with just their eyes.

▼ New stars are forming in this cloud of dark dust and glowing gas in space. It is called the Pelican Nebula.

Families of stars

102 Stars are huge balls of hot gas. They look tiny to us because they are so far away. Deep in the center of a star it is so hot that some of the gas turns into energy. Stars shine by sending out this energy as light and heat.

103 A star starts life in a cloud of dust and gas called a nebula. Thicker parts of the cloud collapse into a ball that becomes a star. Sometimes a star will shine until its gas is used up, and then swell into a red giant star. A large star may then explode as a supernova but smaller ones just shrink, becoming tiny white dwarf stars.

104 A star's color shows how hot it is. Red stars are small and cool, yellow ones are bigger and hotter, and white ones are huge and very hot. Dying stars get even bigger, becoming giants or supergiants.

▶ The Milky Way Galaxy looks like a band of light, instead of a spiral shape, because we are looking through it from inside one of the spiral arms.

BUTTERFLY NEBULA

At the end of its life a red giant star threw out this glowing cloud of gas.

STAR CLUSTER

The Quintuplet cluster is a group of bright young stars. They shine with different colors—red, blue, and white.

ASTRONOMY

M81 GALAXY

This huge spiral galaxy contains billions of stars. Our Milky Way Galaxy would look like this if we could see it from above.

105 After it explodes as a supernova, a giant star may collapse, forming a black hole. The gravity of a black hole is so strong that it pulls everything into it—not even light can escape!

106 Galaxies are huge families of stars. Some are shaped like squashed balls, and these are called elliptical galaxies. Others have a spiral shape with arms curling out from a central ball of stars. Our Sun is in a spiral galaxy called the Milky Way. On very clear, dark nights you can see it as a faint band of light across the sky.

107 Using powerful telescopes, astronomers can see galaxies in all directions. They think there are many billions of galaxies, each containing billions of stars. All these stars and galaxies are part of the Universe. This is the name we give to everything we know about, including all the galaxies, our Sun and Moon, the Earth, and everything on it, including you.

Starry skies

108 People have always been fascinated by the stars and Moon. Ancient people watched the Sun cross the sky during the day and disappear at night. Then when it got dark they saw the Moon and stars move across the sky. They wondered what caused these things to happen.

QUIZ
1. What was the Egyptian sun god called?
2. What did the Chinese see when they thought a dragon was eating the Sun?
3. What was a "long-haired star?"

Answers:
1. Ra 2. An eclipse 3. A comet

109 Sometimes the Sun goes dark in the middle of the day. This is called a solar eclipse, and it is caused by the Moon moving in front of the Sun, blocking its light. People in the past did not know this, so eclipses were scary. In ancient China, people thought they were caused by a dragon eating the Sun.

110 In ancient times people did not know what the Sun, Moon, and stars were. Many thought the Sun was a god. The ancient Egyptians called this god Ra. They believed he rode across the sky in a boat each day and was swallowed by the sky goddess, Nut, every evening and then born again the next morning.

▲ The Egyptians pictured their sky goddess Nut with a starry body and their sun god Ra sitting on a throne.

◀ Ancient Chinese people fired arrows and banged pots and pans during eclipses, believing this would frighten the dragon away.

▶ The Bayeux Tapestry, made during the 1070s, shows people pointing at the famous Halley's comet (at the top right).

◀ The Greek sun god, Helios, rode across the sky in a chariot pulled by horses.

111
Early astronomers could not predict when comets would appear. Comets were known as "long-haired stars" because of their glowing tails, and many people thought they brought bad luck. They were blamed for disasters, from floods and famines to defeat in battle.

▶ Quetzalcoatl was a feathered serpent, and to the Aztec people of Central America he was the god of the morning star.

Mapping the stars

112 Ancient astronomers made maps of star patterns, dividing them into groups called constellations. People around the world all grouped the stars differently. Today, astronomers recognize 88 constellations that cover the whole sky.

▼ The northern half of the Earth has different constellations from the southern half, but all the star patterns stay the same night after night.

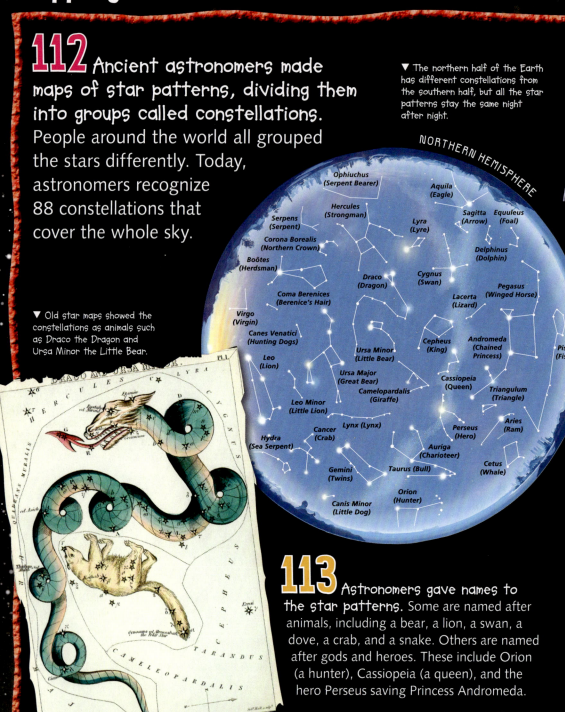

NORTHERN HEMISPHERE

Ophiuchus (Serpent Bearer), Aquila (Eagle), Hercules (Strongman), Sagitta (Arrow), Equuleus (Foal), Serpens (Serpent), Lyra (Lyre), Corona Borealis (Northern Crown), Delphinus (Dolphin), Boötes (Herdsman), Draco (Dragon), Cygnus (Swan), Pegasus (Winged Horse), Lacerta (Lizard), Coma Berenices (Berenice's Hair), Virgo (Virgin), Canes Venatici (Hunting Dogs), Ursa Minor (Little Bear), Cepheus (King), Andromeda (Chained Princess), Pisces (Fishes), Leo (Lion), Ursa Major (Great Bear), Cassiopeia (Queen), Triangulum (Triangle), Camelopardalis (Giraffe), Leo Minor (Little Lion), Lynx (Lynx), Perseus (Hero), Aries (Ram), Cancer (Crab), Hydra (Sea Serpent), Auriga (Charioteer), Gemini (Twins), Taurus (Bull), Cetus (Whale), Canis Minor (Little Dog), Orion (Hunter)

◀ Old star maps showed the constellations as animals such as Draco the Dragon and Ursa Minor the Little Bear.

113 Astronomers gave names to the star patterns. Some are named after animals, including a bear, a lion, a swan, a dove, a crab, and a snake. Others are named after gods and heroes. These include Orion (a hunter), Cassiopeia (a queen), and the hero Perseus saving Princess Andromeda.

ASTRONOMY

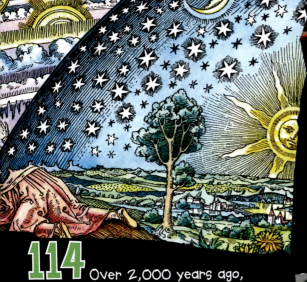

◀ Here an ancient astronomer (bottom left) is pictured comically looking through the starry celestial sphere to see how it moves.

115 **Stars appear to move across the sky at night.** This is because the Earth is spinning all the time, but in the past people thought the stars were fixed to the inside of a huge hollow ball called the celestial sphere, which moved slowly around the Earth.

114 Over 2,000 years ago, the Greek astronomer Hipparchus made a catalog of over 850 stars. He listed their brightness and positions, and called the brightest ones first magnitude stars. Astronomers still call the brightness of a star its magnitude.

SPOT A STAR PATTERN

You will need:
clear night   warm clothes   dark place
good view of the sky

If you live in the North, look for the saucepan-shape of the Big Dipper—four stars for the bowl and three for the handle. If you live in the South, look overhead for four stars in the shape of a cross—the Southern Cross.

SOUTHERN HEMISPHERE

116 Ancient astronomers noticed that one star seems to stay still while the others circle around it. This is the Pole Star. It is above the North Pole and shows which direction is north. The ancient Egyptians used this knowledge to align the sides of the pyramids exactly.

53

Keeping time

117 The Sun, Moon, and stars can be used to measure time. It takes a day for the Earth to spin round, and a year for it to circle the Sun. By observing changes in the positions of constellations, astronomers worked out the length of a year so they could make a calendar.

118 It takes 29.5 days for the Moon to circle the Earth. The Moon seems to change shape because as it moves around Earth, different parts of it are lit by the Sun. When the Sun shines on the side that faces Earth, we see a Full Moon. When the far side is lit the Moon looks dark to us—a New Moon.

▲ The Moon's changing shapes are called the phases of the Moon. It doesn't really change shape—it is always a round ball of rock.

▼ Stonehenge's huge upright stones are lined up with sunrise on the longest day in midsummer and on the shortest day in midwinter.

119 **Ancient people used sundials to tell the time.** A sundial consists of an upright rod and a flat plate. When the Sun shines, the rod casts a shadow on the plate. As the Sun moves across the sky, the shadow moves round the plate. Marks on the plate indicate the hours.

120 **As the Earth circles the Sun, different stars appear in the sky.** This helped people predict when seasons would change. In ancient Egypt the bright star Sirius showed when the river Nile would flood, making the land ready for crops.

121 **Stonehenge is an ancient monument in England that is lined up with the Sun and Moon.** It is a circle of giant stones over 4,000 years old. It may have been used as a calendar, or an observatory to predict when eclipses would happen.

MAKE A SUNDIAL
You will need:
short stick glue cardboard pencil clock

1. Stand the stick upright on the cardboard using the glue. Put it outside on a sunny day.
2. Every hour, make a pencil mark on the cardboard where the shadow ends.
3. Leave the cardboard where it is and the shadow will point to the time whenever the Sun is out.

▼ The shadow made by this sundial points to the time, which is marked on the round dial.

Wandering stars

122 When people began to study the stars they spotted five that were unlike the rest. Instead of staying in fixed patterns, they moved across the constellations, and they did not twinkle. Astronomers called them planets, which means "wandering stars."

123 The planets are named after ancient Roman gods. Mercury is the messenger of the gods, Venus is the god of love, Mars is the god of war, Jupiter is king of the gods, and Saturn is the god of farming. Later astronomers used telescopes to find two more planets, and named them Uranus and Neptune after the gods of the sky and the sea.

124 At first people thought that the Earth was at the center of everything. They believed the Sun, Moon, and planets all circled the Earth. The ancient Greek astronomer Ptolemy thought the Moon was nearest Earth, then Mercury and Venus, then the Sun, and finally Jupiter and Saturn.

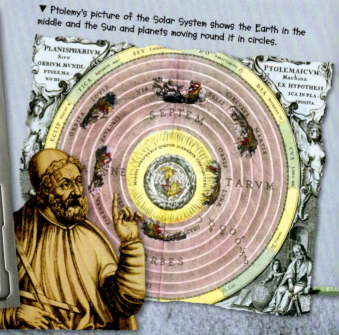

▼ Ptolemy's picture of the Solar System shows the Earth in the middle and the Sun and planets moving round it in circles.

DRAW AN ELLIPSE

You will need:
two thumbtacks   paper
thick cardboard   pencil   string

1. Place the paper on the cardboard. Push the tacks into the paper, placing them a little way apart.
2. Tie the string into a loop that fits loosely round the tacks.
3. Using the pencil point, pull the string tight into a triangle shape.
4. Move the pencil round on the paper, keeping the string tight to draw an ellipse.

125 Astronomers measured the positions and movements of the planets. What they found did not fit Ptolemy's ideas. In 1515, the Polish astronomer Nicolaus Copernicus suggested that the planets circled the Sun. This explained much of what the astronomers saw, but still didn't fit the measurements exactly.

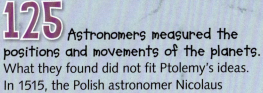

◀ Nicolaus Copernicus' view placed the Sun in the middle with the Earth moving round it with the other planets.

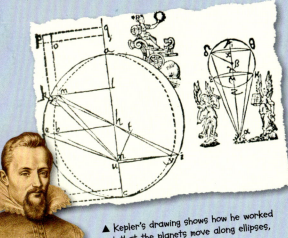

▲ Kepler's drawing shows how he worked out that the planets move along ellipses, not circles.

126 German astronomer Johannes Kepler published his solution to this problem in 1609. He realized that the orbits of Earth and the planets were not perfect circles, but ellipses (slightly squashed circles). This fit all the measurements and describes the Solar System as we know it today.

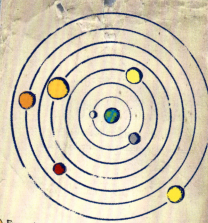

① From above, Ptolemy's plan shows everything (from inside to outside: Earth's Moon, Mercury, Venus, Sun, Mars, Jupiter, Saturn) moving round the Earth.

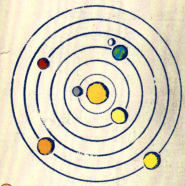

② Copernicus' view changes this to show everything moving round the Sun.

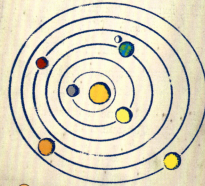

③ Kepler changes the circular paths of the planets into ellipses.

First telescopes

127 The telescope was invented in about 1608. Telescopes use two lenses (disks of glass that bulge out in the middle, or curve inward)—one at each end of a tube. When you look through a telescope, distant things look nearer and larger.

128 Italian scientist Galileo built a telescope in 1609. He was one of the first people to use the new invention for astronomy. With it, Galileo observed craters and mountains on the Moon, and discovered four moons circling the planet Jupiter. He was also amazed to see many more stars in the sky.

▲ Galileo shows a crowd of people the exciting new things he can see through his telescope.

Mirror

JUPITER

IO

EUROPA

CALLISTO

GANYMEDE

▲ Jupiter's four largest moons are called the Galilean moons, because Galileo was the first person to see them using his telescope.

129 When Galileo looked at the planet Venus through his telescope he saw that it sometimes appeared to be crescent shaped, just like the Moon. This meant that Venus was circling the Sun and not the Earth and helped to prove that Copernicus was right about the planets circling the Sun. Galileo described his amazing discoveries in a book called *The Starry Messenger*.

ASTRONOMY

130 **Other astronomers were soon trying to build more powerful telescopes.** In 1668, English scientist Isaac Newton made one in which he replaced one of the lenses with a curved mirror, shaped like a saucer. He had invented the reflecting telescope. Large modern telescopes are based on Newton's invention.

131 **According to legend, Newton began to think about gravity when he saw an apple fall from a tree.** He wondered why the apple fell down to the ground instead of floating upward.

132 **Newton also worked out why the planets orbit the Sun.** He realized that something was pulling the planets toward the Sun—a pulling force called gravity. The pull of the Sun's gravity keeps the planets in their orbits, and the Earth's gravity holds the Moon in its orbit. It also prevents everything on Earth from floating off into space.

◀ The mirror in Newton's telescope gave a clearer image of the stars than telescopes with lenses.

Eyepiece
Sliding focus
Ball mounting

Discoveries with telescopes

▶ Halley's comet was last seen in 1986 and will return again in 2061.

133 Astronomers made many new discoveries with their telescopes. The English astronomer Edmund Halley was interested in comets. He thought that a bright comet seen in 1682 was the same as one that was seen in 1607, and predicted that it would return in 1758. His prediction was right and the comet was named after him—Halley's Comet.

◀ Halley also mapped the stars and studied the Sun and Moon.

▼ The Orion Nebula, a huge glowing cloud of gas, is Messier's object number 42.

134 The French astronomer Charles Messier was also a comet hunter. In 1781 he tried to make his search easier by listing over 100 fuzzy objects in the sky that could be mistaken for comets. Later astronomers realized that some of these are glowing clouds of dust and gas and others are distant galaxies.

▲ Messier's object number 16 is the Eagle Nebula, a dusty cloud where stars are born.

▼ Messier's object number 31 is a giant spiral galaxy called Andromeda.

ASTRONOMY

135 William Herschel, a German astronomer living in England, discovered a new planet in 1781. Using a reflecting telescope he had built himself, he spotted a star that seemed to move. It didn't look like a comet, and Herschel realized that it must be a new planet. It was the first planet discovered with a telescope and was called Uranus.

▲ William Herschel worked as astronomer for King George III of England.

136 Astronomers soon discovered that Uranus was not following its expected orbit. They thought another planet might be pulling it off course. Following predictions made by mathematicians, astronomers found another planet in 1846. It was called Neptune. It is so far away that it looks like a star.

137 The discovery of Neptune didn't fully explain Uranus' orbit. In 1930 an American astronomer, Clyde Tombaugh, found Pluto. It was the ninth planet from the Sun and much smaller than expected. In 2006 astronomers decided to call Pluto a dwarf planet.

▲ Herschel's great telescope was the largest telescope in the world at the time and its mirror measured 4 feet across.

QUIZ

1. Who discovered the planet Uranus?
2. When was Halley's Comet last seen?
3. Which was the ninth planet from the Sun until 2006?

Answers:
1. William Herschel 2. 1986 3. Pluto

How telescopes work

138 **Telescopes make distant things look nearer.** Most stars are so far away that even with a telescope they just look like points of light. But the Moon and planets seem much larger through a telescope—you can see details such as craters on the Moon and cloud patterns on Jupiter.

139 **A reflecting telescope uses a curved mirror to collect light.** The mirror reflects and focuses the light. A second, smaller mirror sends the light out through the side of the telescope or back through a hole in the big mirror to an eyepiece lens. Looking through the eyepiece lens you see a larger image of the distant object.

▶ Star light bounces off the main mirror of a reflecting telescope back up to the eyepiece lens near the top.

140 **A telescope that uses a lens instead of a mirror to collect light is called a refracting telescope.** The lens focuses the light and it goes straight down the telescope tube to the eyepiece lens at the other end. Refracting telescopes are not as large as reflecting ones because large lenses are very heavy.

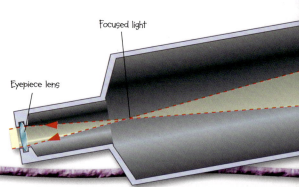

141 Astronomers are building telescopes with larger and larger mirrors. Bigger mirrors reveal fainter objects so telescopes can see further and further into the Universe. They also show more details in the distant galaxies and the wispy glowing clouds between the stars.

142 Today, professional astronomers don't look through their telescopes. They use cameras to capture the images. A camera can build up an image over a long time. The light adds up to make a brighter image, showing things that could not be seen by just looking through the telescope.

▲ A telescope reveals round craters on the Moon and large dark patches called "seas" although the Moon is completely dry.

▲ The mirror from the Rosse Telescope in Ireland is 6 feet across and is kept in the Science Museum in London. One hundred years ago it was the largest telescope in the world.

▼ In a refracting telescope the main lens at the top bends the light, making an image near the bottom of the telescope.

Primary lens

Light enters

I DON'T BELIEVE IT!
The Liverpool telescope on the island of La Palma in the Atlantic Ocean is able to automatically observe a list of objects sent to it via the Internet.

Telescopes today

143 All large modern telescopes are reflecting telescopes. To make clear images, their mirrors must be exactly the right shape. The mirrors are made of polished glass, covered with a thin layer of aluminum to reflect as much light as possible. Some are made of thin glass that would sag without supports beneath to hold it in exactly the right shape.

144 Large telescope mirrors are often made up of many smaller mirrors. The mirrors of the Keck telescopes in Hawaii are made of 36 separate parts. Each has six sides, which fit together to make a mirror 33 feet across—about the width of a tennis court. The small mirrors are tilted to make exactly the right shape.

145 The air above a telescope is constantly moving. This can make their images blurred. Astronomers reduce this by using an extra mirror that can change shape. A computer works out what shape this mirror needs to be to remove the blurring effect and keeps changing it every few seconds. This is called adaptive optics.

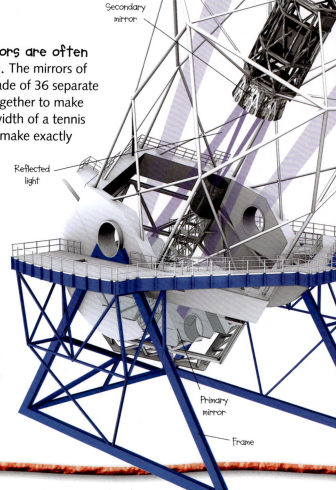

▶ A huge frame holds the mirrors of a large reflecting telescope in position while tilting and turning to point at the stars.

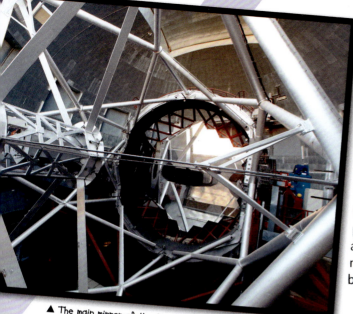

▲ The main mirror of the Gran Telescopio Canarias telescope measures 34 feet across when all its 36 separate parts are fitted together.

146 Large telescopes can work together to see finer detail than a single telescope. When the two Keck telescopes are linked, they produce images that are almost as good as a telescope with a mirror as wide as the distance between them—280 feet.

147 Telescopes must be able to move to track the stars. It may take hours to make an image of a very faint, distant target and during this time the target will move gradually across the sky. Motors drive the telescope at just the right speed to keep it pointing at the target. All the time the image is being recorded.

QUIZ

1. What are telescope mirrors made of?
2. How many sides does each piece of a Keck telescope mirror have?
3. Why do telescopes have to move?

Answers:
1. Glass 2. 6 3. To track the stars

▶ This picture of Saturn was taken by one of the Keck telescopes. The orange colors have been added to show the different temperatures in its clouds and rings.

Observatories

148 Observatories are places for watching the skies, often where telescopes are built and housed. There are usually several telescopes of different sizes at one observatory. Astronomers choose remote places far from cities, as bright lights can spoil observations.

TRUE OR FALSE?
1. Observatories are built close to large cities for convenience.
2. The volcano that the Mauna Kea observatory is built on is dormant.
3. Chile is a good place to build observatories because it rains a lot.

Answers:
1. False 2. True 3. False

149 Observatories are often on the tops of mountains and in dry desert areas. This is because the air close to the ground is constantly moving and full of clouds and dust. Astronomers need very clear, dry, still air so they build their telescopes as high as possible above most of the clouds and dust.

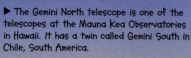

▶ The Gemini North telescope is one of the telescopes at the Mauna Kea Observatories in Hawaii. It has a twin called Gemini South in Chile, South America.

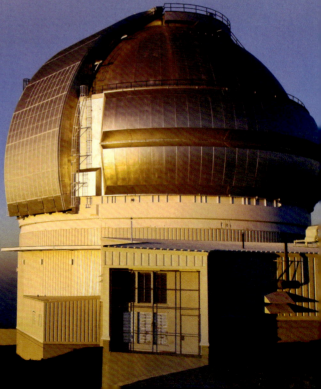

150 **A desert is a good place to build an observatory.** The high mountains in the Atacama Desert, in Chile, South America, are among the driest places on Earth, and night skies there are incredibly dark. Several large telescopes have been built there including the Very Large Telescope (VLT).

▲ The Very Large Telescope is really four large telescopes and four smaller ones. The large telescopes are inside the square domes.

151 **Some famous observatories are on top of a dormant volcano called Mauna Kea, on the island of Hawaii.** It is the highest mountain on an island in the world—most clouds are below it. It is a good place for astronomy because the air is very clean and dry. It has more clear nights than most other places on Earth. It has 13 telescopes, four of them very large.

Telescope inside

Raised shutter

Rotating dome

Building linking telescopes

▲ The two Keck telescopes at the Mauna Kea Observatories each have their own round dome with shutters that open to let in the starlight.

▼ Observatories on Mauna Kea, Hawaii.

The Keck telescopes

152 **Domes cover the telescopes to protect them and keep the mirrors clean.** The domes have shutters that open when the telescopes are operating to let in the starlight. They also turn round so that the telescope can point in any direction and can move to track the stars.

Splitting light

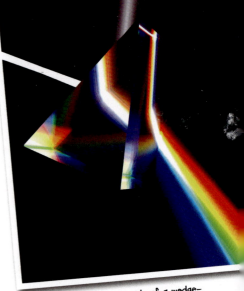

153 Astronomers find out about distant stars by studying the starlight that reaches Earth. They can get more data from the light by splitting it into its different colors—like a rainbow that forms when raindrops split up sunlight. These colors are called a spectrum.

▲ White light going in one side of a wedge-shaped glass prism spreads out into a rainbow of colors, making a spectrum.

RAINBOW SPECTRUM
You will need:
drinking glass   small mirror
water   flashlight   cardboard

1. Put the mirror in the glass so that it faces upward.
2. Pour water into the glass to cover the mirror.
3. In a dark room, shine the flashlight onto the mirror.
4. Hold the cardboard to catch the reflected light from the mirror and see a rainbow—the water and mirror have split the light into a spectrum.

154 Astronomers can tell how hot a star is from its spectrum. The hottest are blue-white, the coolest are red, and in between are yellow and orange stars. The spectrum also shows how big and bright the star is so astronomers can tell which are ordinary stars and which are red giants or supergiants.

155 A star's spectrum can show what gases the star is made of. Each gas has a different pattern of lines in the spectrum. Astronomers can also use the spectrum to find out which different gases make up a cloud of gas, by looking at starlight that has traveled through the cloud.

▶ Astronomers divide stars into classes from O, largest and hottest, to M, smallest and coolest.

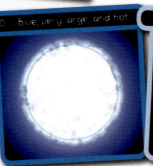
O Blue, very large and hot

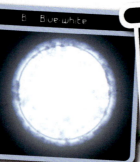
B Blue-white

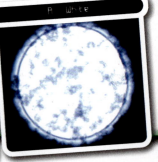
A White

156 If a star or galaxy is moving away from Earth, its light is stretched out. This shows up in its spectrum and astronomers call it red shift. They use it to work out how fast a galaxy is moving and how far away it is. If the galaxy is moving toward Earth, the light gets squashed together and shows up in its spectrum as blue shift.

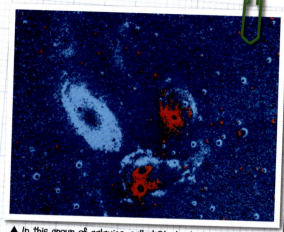

▲ In this group of galaxies, called Stephan's Quintet, the ones that have been colored red are moving away very quickly.

▼ This diagram shows the light waves coming to Earth from a distant galaxy as a wiggly line.

① A galaxy that stays the same distance from us has a normal spectrum.

② If the galaxy is moving away the light is stretched out and the spectrum shifts toward the red end.

③ If the galaxy is moving nearer, the light is squashed up and the spectrum shifts toward the blue end.

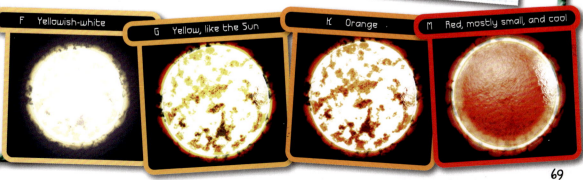

F Yellowish-white
G Yellow, like the Sun
K Orange
M Red, mostly small, and cool

Space telescopes

CRAB NEBULA

157 Galaxies and stars send out other kinds of radiation, as well as light. Some send out radio waves like the ones that carry TV signals. There are also X-rays, like the kind that hospitals use to show broken bones, infrared light, gamma rays, and ultra-violet light. They all carry information.

159 The Hubble Space Telescope is like a normal telescope, but it is above the air. Its images are much clearer than if it were on the ground. It has produced images of distant gas clouds showing star birth, and looked deep into space at galaxies that have never been seen before.

▶ The Hubble Space Telescope was launched into orbit around the Earth in 1990 and is still sending astronomers amazing images from space.

158 Some kinds of radiation are detected more easily by telescopes in space. This is because the air around Earth stops most radiation from reaching the ground, which is good, because it would be harmful to life on Earth. Space telescopes orbit Earth to collect the radiation and send the information down to Earth.

QUIZ
1. What kind of radiation can spot newborn stars?
2. Which space telescopes collect gamma rays from space?
3. What kind of radiation can spot black holes?

Answers:
1. Infrared radiation 2. The Fermi and Integral Gamma-ray Telescopes 3. X-rays and gamma rays

ASTRONOMY

This picture includes data from Hubble (colored green and dark blue), Spitzer (colored red), and Chandra (colored pale blue).

160 **The space telescopes Chandra X-ray Observatory and XMM Newton both collect X-rays.** The X-rays come from very hot gas inside huge galaxy clusters. They also reveal black holes, because gas swirling around black holes gets so hot that it gives out X-rays.

◀ For over 20 years the Chandra X-ray Observatory has orbited the Earth looking at black holes and exploding stars.

161 **The Spitzer and Herschel space telescopes, now retired, picked up infrared light.** Infrared comes from cool stars and clouds of dust and gas. It can be used to see through dust clouds around newborn stars, and around young stars where new planets may be forming. It also reveals the center of our galaxy, which is hidden by dust.

▶ The Spitzer space telescope had to be kept very cold so it could pick out the infrared light from distant galaxies.

162 **The Fermi Gamma-ray Space Telescope and Integral are telescopes that collect gamma rays.** These rays come from violent events in space such as huge explosions when stars blow up or collide. Like X-rays, gamma rays can also reveal black holes.

Radio telescopes

163 Radio waves from space are collected by radio telescopes. Most radio waves can travel through the air, so these telescopes are built on the ground. But there are lots of radio waves traveling around the Earth, carrying TV and radio signals, and phone calls. These can all interfere with the faint radio waves from space.

164 Radio telescopes work like reflecting telescopes, but instead of using a mirror, waves are collected by a big metal dish. They look like huge satellite TV aerials. Most dishes can turn to point at targets anywhere in the sky, and can track targets moving across the sky.

▶ Each radio telescope dish in the Very Large Array measures 82 feet across and can tilt and turn to face in different directions.

165 Some scientists use radio telescopes to listen out for messages from aliens on other planets or in other galaxies. They have not found any yet.

166 We can't see radio waves, but astronomers turn the signals into images we can see. The images from a single radio telescope dish are not very detailed but several radio telescopes linked together can reveal finer details. The Very Large Array (VLA) in New Mexico, has 27 separate dishes arranged in a "Y" shape, all working together as though it was one huge dish 22.5 miles across.

▶ These two orange blobs are clouds of hot gas on either side of a galaxy. They are invisible to ordinary telescopes but radio telescopes can reveal them.

167 Radio waves come from cool gas between the stars. This gas is not hot enough to glow so it can't be seen by ordinary telescopes. Radio telescopes have mapped clouds of gas showing the shape of the Milky Way Galaxy. They have also discovered what seems to be a massive black hole at its center.

168 Radio waves reveal massive jets of gas shooting out from distant galaxies. The jets are thrown out by giant black holes in the middle of some galaxies, which are gobbling up stars and gas around them.

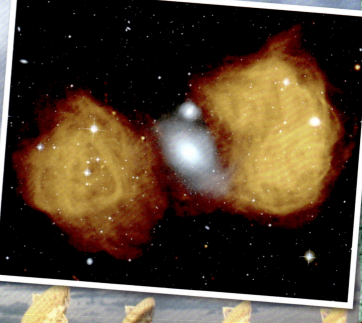

Watching the Sun

169 **The Sun is our closest star and astronomers study it to learn about other stars.** Without the Sun's light and heat nothing could live on the Earth, so astronomers keep a close eye on it. Tongues of very hot gas called flares and prominences often shoot out from the Sun.

▼ A loop of glowing gas called a prominence ❶ arches away from the Sun. Sun spots ❷ look dark because they are cooler than the rest of the surface.

170 **Particles constantly stream out from the surface of the Sun in all directions.** This is called the solar wind. Sometimes a huge burst of particles, called a Coronal Mass Ejection (CME), breaks out. If one comes toward Earth it could damage satellites and even telephone and power lines. CMEs can be dangerous for astronauts in space.

171 **There are often dark patches on the Sun.** These are cooler areas, and are called sunspots. The number of sunspots changes over time. Every 11 years numbers increase to a maximum of 100 or more, then in between the numbers go down to very few, or even none.

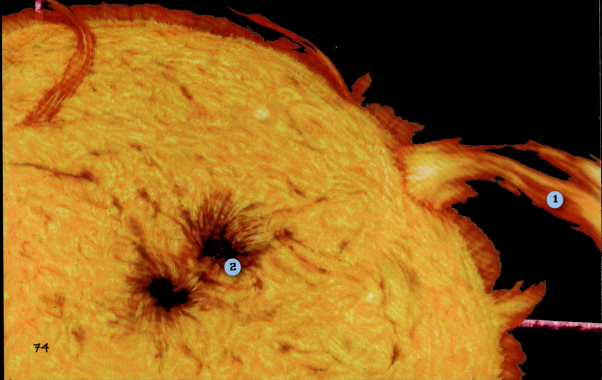

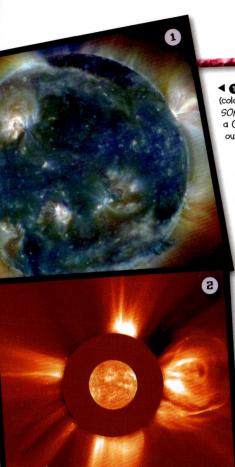

◀ ❶ Wispy gas surrounds the Sun (colored blue) in this image from the SOHO spacecraft. ❷ SOHO captures a Coronal Mass Ejection exploding out from the Sun.

WARNING
Never look directly at the Sun, especially not through a telescope or binoculars. It is so bright it will harm your eyes and could even make you blind.

172 A spacecraft called SOHO has been watching the Sun since 1995. It orbits the Sun between the Earth and the Sun, sending data and images back to Earth. It warns of changes in solar wind and of CMEs that could hit Earth, and has spotted many comets crashing into the Sun.

173 The Sun is losing weight! Every second, about 4.5 million tons of its gas is turned into energy and escapes as light and heat. The Sun is so big that it can continue losing weight at this rate for about another 5 billion years.

174 STEREO are a pair of spacecraft that look at the Sun. They orbit the Sun, one each side of the Earth, to get a 3D view. Like SOHO, they are looking for storms on the Sun that could affect the Earth. Information from STEREO is helping astronomers to work out why these storms happen.

▶ This illustration shows the two STEREO spacecraft soon after they were launched in 2006. They moved apart until they were on either side of the Earth.

75

The edge of the Universe

175 **Astronomers think that the Universe started in a huge explosion they call the Big Bang.** They know that distant galaxies are all moving further apart so the Universe must have been squashed tightly together billions of years ago. They think that some kind of explosion sent everything flying apart about 13.7 billion years ago.

176 **As astronomers look farther away they are also looking back in time.** This is because light takes time to travel across the vast distances in space. It takes over four years for light to reach Earth from the second-nearest star (after the Sun), so we see this star as it was when the light left it four years ago. Light can take billions of years to travel from distant galaxies, so astronomers are looking back at the Universe as it was billions of years ago.

④ Our Sun and the Solar System formed after about 9 billion years.

③ Stars and galaxies appeared after about 200–600 million years.

② After 300,000 years atoms started to form.

① The Universe was unimaginably hot and tiny at first but cooled as it expanded.

9 billion yrs

300 million yrs

300,000 yrs

▶ This shows the Universe as it expanded and changed from the Big Bang to the present day.

ASTRONOMY

◀ A map of the Cosmic Background Radiation shows tiny differences in temperature. The red areas are slightly warmer and the blue areas cooler.

177 **Astronomers have found faint radiation coming from all over the sky.** They call this the Cosmic Background Radiation. It is the remains of radiation left by the Big Bang explosion and helps to prove that the Big Bang really happened. Astronomers send satellites up to map this radiation and find out more about the Universe when it was very young.

13.7 billion yrs

● The Universe is now about 13.7 billion years old.

▲ These galaxies are so far away that we are seeing them as they were billions of years ago when the Universe was much younger.

178 **Astronomers use their biggest telescopes and space telescopes to try and find the most distant galaxies.** They do not know how soon after the Big Bang the first stars and galaxies appeared and whether they were different from the stars and galaxies they see today. The Hubble Space Telescope has taken images of very faint faraway galaxies showing astronomers what the early Universe was like.

Up close

QUIZ

1. How many planets did the Voyager 2 space probe visit?
2. Did the *Spirit* and *Opportunity* rovers find running water on Mars?
3. How did the *Magellan* space probe map Venus?

Answers:
1. Four 2. No—but they found signs that there may have been some long ago 3. It used radar to "see" through the clouds

179 The planets and our Moon have all been explored by space probes. These travel through space carrying cameras and other instruments with which they can gather data. They then send all the information and images back to astronomers on Earth.

180 Some space probes fly past planets, gathering information. The *Voyager 2* space probe flew past the four giant planets (Jupiter, Saturn, Uranus, and Neptune) in turn between 1979 and 1989. Astronomers now know much more about these planets from the detailed information and images *Voyager 2* sent back.

VOYAGER 2

▶ Voyager 2 sent back this picture of Callisto, one of Jupiter's large moons.

Launch date: August 20, 1977
Mission: Flew past Jupiter in 1979, Saturn in 1981, Uranus in 1986, and Neptune in 1989. It continued on, leaving the Solar System in 2018.

ASTRONOMY

181 **Space probes can orbit a planet to study it for longer.** The probe *Cassini* went into orbit around Saturn. It carried a smaller probe that dropped onto Saturn's largest moon, Titan, to look at its surface, which is hidden by cloud. The main probe circled Saturn, investigating its moons and rings.

182 **Venus is hidden by clouds, but the *Magellan* probe was able to map its surface.** The probe sent radio signals through the clouds to bounce off the surface. It then collected the return signal. This is called radar. It revealed that Venus has many volcanoes.

CASSINI

▶ Saturn and its rings, taken by the *Cassini* spacecraft as it approached the planet.

Launch date: October 15, 1997
Mission: Arrived at Saturn in 2004. Dropped *Huygens* probe onto Saturn's largest moon, Titan, then went into orbit to explore Saturn, its rings, and moons.

SPIRIT AND OPPORTUNITY

183 **Some probes land on a planet's surface.** The probes *Spirit* and *Opportunity* explored the surface of Mars. They moved slowly, stopping to take pictures and analyze rocks. They discovered that although Mars is very dry now, there was once water on the surface.

Launch date: June 10, 2003 (*Spirit*) and July 7, 2003 (*Opportunity*)
Mission: After landing on Mars in January 2004 the two rovers drove across the surface testing the rocks and soil and sending back images and data.

▲ Among the many rocks scattered across the dusty Martian landscape *Spirit* found a rock that could have crashed down from space.

Astronomy from home

184 Many people enjoy astronomy as a hobby. You need warm clothes and somewhere dark, away from street and house lights, and a clear night. After about half an hour your eyes adjust to the dark so you can see more stars. A map of the constellations will help you find your way around the night sky.

185 Binoculars reveal even more stars and show details on the Moon. It is best to look at the Moon when it is half full. Craters, where rocks have crashed into the Moon, show up along the dark edge down the middle of the Moon. Binoculars also show Jupiter's moons as spots of light on or either side of the planet.

186 Telescopes are usually more powerful than binoculars and show fainter stars. They also show more detail in faint gas clouds called nebulae. Amateurs use reflecting and refracting telescopes, mounted on stands to keep them steady.

187 A camera can be fixed to a telescope to photograph the sky. A camera can build up an image over time if the telescope moves to follow the stars. The images show details that you could not see by just looking through the telescope.

KIT LIST
- Star map
- Red light flashlight
- Deckchair
- Warm clothes
- Pencil and notebook
- Blanket or sleeping bag
- Binoculars
- Telescope

SPOT VENUS

Venus is the brightest planet and easy to spot—it is known as the "evening star." Look toward the west in the twilight just after the Sun has set. The first bright "star" to appear will often be Venus.

ASTRONOMY

▼ In November each year amateur astronomers look out for extra shooting stars during the Leonid meteor shower.

▲ In 1997 the bright Comet Hale Bopp could be seen easily without a telescope or binoculars.

188 **Meteors, also called shooting stars, look like streaks of light in the sky.** They are made when tiny pieces of space rock and dust hit the air around the Earth and burn up. Several times during the year there are meteor showers when many shooting stars are seen. You can spot meteors without a telescope or binoculars.

189 **Amateurs can collect useful information for professional astronomers.** They are often the first to spot a new comet in the sky. Comets are named after the person who found them and some amateur astronomers even specialize in comet-spotting. Others watch variable stars and keep records of the changes in their brightness.

▶ An amateur astronomer uses binoculars to see the many stars in the Milky Way.

Past, present, and future

190 Kepler was a space telescope built to look for exoplanets—planets that orbit stars outside our Solar System. Kepler's observations led to the discovery of over 2,600 worlds. In 2018 it was replaced by the Transiting Exoplanet Survey Satellite, which has continued to study exoplanets.

▶ A *Delta II* rocket launches the Kepler spacecraft in March 2009 on its mission to hunt for distant planets.

I DON'T BELIEVE IT!
Astronomers are planning a new radio telescope, to be built in either Australia or South Africa. It is called the Square Kilometer Array and will have at least 3,000 separate radio telescopes. It should start working in the 2020s.

191 ALMA (short for Atacama Large Millimeter Array) is a powerful new radio telescope built high up in the Atacama Desert in Chile. It has 66 radio dishes linked together to make one huge radio telescope and began scientific observations in 2011.

ASTRONOMY

192 **The James Webb Space Telescope was launched in 2021.** It is an infrared telescope that will build on Hubble's discoveries by looking inside dust clouds to where stars and planets are forming. Its mirror is 21 feet across, made up of 18 separate mirrors that fit together. Having such a big mirror means it can collect more light, allowing it to see even further.

▲ A large sunshield keeps the mirrors of the James Webb Telescope cool so it can make images using infrared light.

193 **Several new giant telescopes are being planned.** The Thirty Meter Telescope will have a mirror 30 meters (98 feet) across—about the length of two school buses. This will be made of 492 smaller mirrors. The European Extremely Large Telescope will have an even larger mirror, 138 feet across, made of 984 separate mirrors.

▲ The European Extremely Large Telescope will be the largest optical telescope in the world when it is built in the Atacama Desert in Chile.

194 **A new weather-tracking satellite is being tested in Earth's orbit.** GOES-18 (Geostationary Operational Environmental Satellite) is the third of four new satellites and will provide more accurate weather forecasts and storm predictions.

EXPLORING SPACE

195 **For thousands of years people gazed up at the night sky and wondered what it would be like to explore space.** This became a reality around 60 years ago, and since then humans have been to the Moon, and unmanned spacecraft have visited all of the planets in the Solar System. Spacecraft have also explored other planets' moons, asteroids, and glowing comets. These amazing discoveries help us to understand the Universe.

▶ ESA's INTEGRAL satellite (launched in 2002) is deployed from a Proton rocket to observe invisible gamma rays in space. Since 1957, humans have sent spacecraft to all eight planets in the Solar System, as well as more than 50 moons, asteroids, and comets.

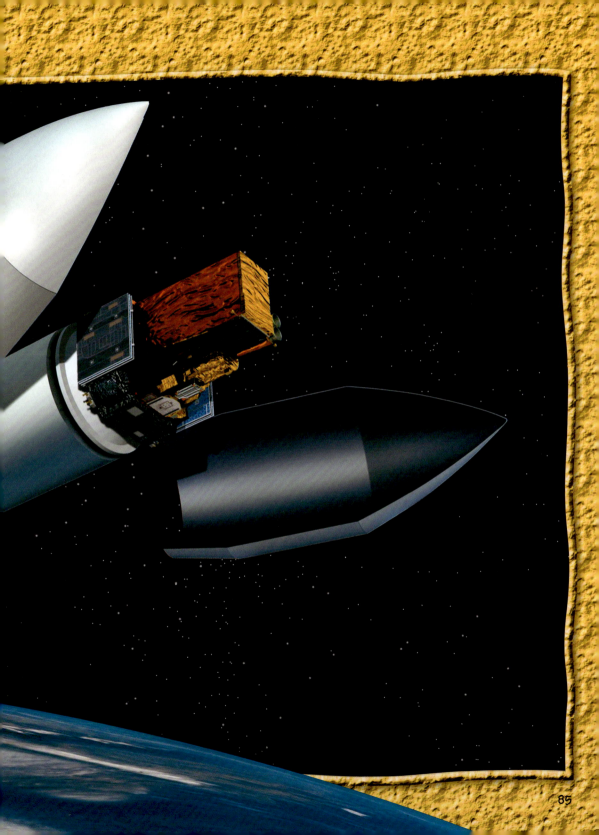

Who explores, and why?

196 Exploring space involves sending craft, robots, equipment, and sometimes people to planets, moons, asteroids, and comets. Some craft fly near to their targets, while others land. As they explore, they gather information to send back to Earth.

197 Space exploration is different from other space sciences. For example, astronomy is the study of objects in space including planets, stars, and galaxies, as well as the Universe as a whole. Much of this is done using telescopes, rather than traveling out into space.

198 The *Cassini-Huygens* mission to Saturn is one of the most expensive missions ever. It cost over $3.3 billion—the price of 12 Airbus A380 super jumbo jets.

Vandenberg Air Force Base and Spaceport, California, USA

NASA Headquarters, Washington D.C., USA

Kennedy Space Center, Florida, USA

Alcântara Launch Center, São Luís, Brazil

Guiana Space Center, Kourou, French Guiana

▲ Space mission headquarters and launch sites are spread across the world.

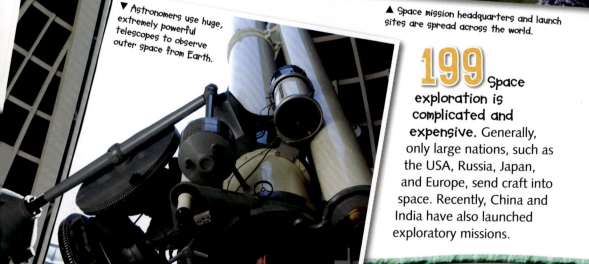

▼ Astronomers use huge, extremely powerful telescopes to observe outer space from Earth.

199 Space exploration is complicated and expensive. Generally, only large nations, such as the USA, Russia, Japan, and Europe, send craft into space. Recently, China and India have also launched exploratory missions.

200 **Sending even a small spacecraft into space costs vast amounts of money.** The Japanese *Hayabusa* mission to bring back samples of the comet Itokawa began in 2003. It lasted seven years and cost around $170 million. Sending the *Phoenix* lander to Mars in 2008 was even more expensive, at $450 million.

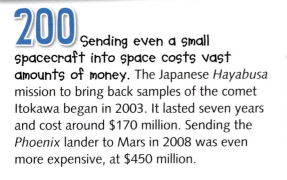

▶ The comet-visiting *Hayabusa* spacecraft blasted off from Uchinoura Space Center, Japan, in 2003. It returned to Earth in 2010, carrying samples of comet dust.

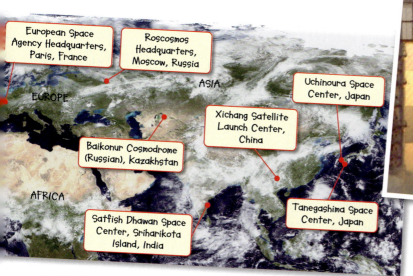

European Space Agency Headquarters, Paris, France

Roscosmos Headquarters, Moscow, Russia

ASIA

EUROPE

Uchinoura Space Center, Japan

Xichang Satellite Launch Center, China

Baikonur Cosmodrome (Russian), Kazakhstan

AFRICA

Satish Dhawan Space Center, Sriharikota Island, India

Tanegashima Space Center, Japan

▼ Recent observations in space show faraway stars have planets forming around them from bits of gas, dust, and rock—similiar to our own Solar System.

201 **If the costs are so great, why do we explore space?** Exploring the unknown has long been a part of human nature. Space exploration provides clues that may help us to understand how the Universe formed. Progress in space technology can also help advances on Earth.

Early explorers

202 The Space Age began in 1957 when Russia launched Sputnik 1, the first Earth-orbiting satellite. It was a metal, ball-shaped craft that could measure pressure and temperature, and send radio signals back to Earth.

▼ Tracking Sputnik 1's orbit showed how the upper atmosphere of the Earth fades into space.

203 In 1958, the U.S. launched the satellite Explorer 1. As it orbited the Earth it detected two donut-shaped belts of high-energy particles, known as the Van Allen Belts. They can damage spacecraft and interfere with radio signals.

▼ The Van Allen belts are made up of particles, trapped by Earth's natural magnetic field.

Inner belt
Outer belt

Heat-resistant outer casing.
Inner casing.
Batteries.
Antennae.
Ventilation fan.

204 In 1959, Russia's *Luna 1* spacecraft was aiming for the Moon, but it missed. Later that year, *Luna 2* crashed into the Moon on purpose, becoming the first craft to reach another world. On its way down the craft measured the Moon's gravity and magnetism.

QUIZ
Early exploration was a "Space Race" between the U.S. and the Soviet Union. Which had these "firsts?"
1. First satellite in space.
2. First person in space.
3. First craft on the Moon.
4. First person on the Moon.

Answers:
1, 2, 3—Russia 4—U.S.A.

Hatch.

Heat shield covering.

Long range antenna.

◀ Gagarin's *Vostok 1* spacecraft was ten times larger than the *Sputnik 1* satellite, and 50 times heavier.

Descent module— only this ball-shaped part came back to Earth.

Oxygen and nitrogen gas tanks for fuel and for Gagarin to breathe.

Retro-thruster.

205
The first person in space was Russian cosmonaut Yuri Gagarin. In 1961 he made one orbit of Earth in the spacecraft *Vostok 1*. The furthest he traveled into space was 203 miles. Gagarin's trip made news around the world and showed that humans could survive in space.

206
The U.S. sent seven Surveyor craft to the Moon between 1966 and 1968. Five succeeded in soft-landing (landing without being destroyed) on the surface. This was an important stage in planning the most exciting and ambitious mission of all—sending people to another world.

▶ *Surveyor 3* landed on the Moon in April 1967. It was photographed by the *Apollo 12* astronauts in November 1969.

89

Man on the Moon

207 The only humans to have explored another world are 12 U.S. astronauts that were part of the Apollo program. Six Apollo missions landed on the Moon between 1969 and 1972, each with two astronauts. First to step onto the surface were Neil Armstrong and Buzz Aldrin from *Apollo 11*, on July 20, 1969.

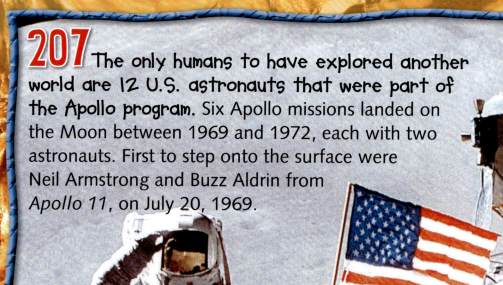

208 Each Apollo lunar lander touched down on a different type of terrain. The astronauts stayed on the Moon for three or four days. They explored, carried out experiments, and collected samples of Moon dust and rocks to bring back to Earth.

209 The last three Apollo missions took a Lunar Roving Vehicle (LRV), or "Moon buggy." The astronauts drove for up to 12 miles at a time, exploring the Moon's hills, valleys, flat plains, and cliffs.

EXPLORING SPACE

210
Since the Apollo missions, more than 50 unmanned spacecraft have orbited or landed on the Moon. In 1994, U.S. orbiter *Clementine* took many photographs, gravity readings, and detailed maps of the Moon's surface.

◀ *Apollo 15*'s Lunar Module pilot James Irwin salutes the U.S. flag and his Commander David Scott, in 1971. Their Lunar Module lander is behind and the Moon buggy is to the right.

211
In 2009, the *Lunar Reconnaissance Orbiter* began mapping the Moon's surface in detail. Its pictures showed parts of the Apollo craft left by the astronauts. In the same year the Indian orbiter *Chandrayaan 1* discovered ice on the Moon.

◀ On each mission, the Commander (C) and the Lunar Module pilot (LMP) landed on the Moon, while the Command Module pilot (CMP) stayed in the orbiting craft.

MISSION	DATE	CREW	ACHIEVEMENT
Apollo 11	July 1969	Neil Armstrong (C) Buzz Aldrin (LMP) Michael Collins (CMP)	First humans on another world.
Apollo 12	November 1969	Pete Conrad (C) Alan Bean (LMP) Richard Gordon (CMP)	First color television pictures of the Moon returned to Earth.
Apollo 13	April 1970	James Lovell (C) Fred Haise (LMP) Jack Swigert (CMP)	Apollo 13 turned back after launch because of an explosion. It never reached the Moon, but returned safely to Earth.
Apollo 14	January–February 1971	Alan Shepard (C) Edgar Mitchell (LMP) Stuart Roosa (CMP)	Longest Moon walks in much improved spacesuits.
Apollo 15	July–August 1971	David Scott (C) James Irwin (LMP) Alfred Worden (CMP)	First use of a Moon buggy allowed astronauts to explore a wider range.
Apollo 16	April 1972	John Young (C) Charles Duke (LMP) Thomas Mattingly (CMP)	First and only mission to land in the Moon's highlands.
Apollo 17	December 1972	Eugene Cernan (C) Harrison Schmitt (LMP) Ronald Evans (CMP)	Returned a record 108 pounds of rock and dust samples.

Plan and prepare

212 Planning a mission takes many years. Scientists suggest places to explore, what might be discovered, and the cost. Their government must agree for the mission to go ahead.

▲ In 1961 U.S. space engineer John Houbolt developed the idea of using a three-part spacecraft for the Apollo Moon missions.

213 There are many types of exploratory missions. A flyby takes the spacecraft near to its target world, and past. An orbiter circles around the target. A lander mission touches down on the surface. A lander may release a rover, which can travel around on the surface.

▲ For worlds with an atmosphere, parachutes are used to lower a lander gently. This parachute design for a planned mission to Mars is being tested in the world's biggest wind tunnel in California.

214 The ever-changing positions of Earth and other objects in space mean there is a limited "launch window" for each mission. This is when Earth is in the best position for a craft to reach its target in the shortest time. If the launch window is missed, the distances may become too massive.

215 In space, repairs are difficult or impossible. Exploring craft must be incredibly reliable, with tested and proven technology. Each piece of equipment needs a back-up, and even if this fails, it should not affect other parts.

▼ The *New Horizons* spacecraft was assembled and checked in perfectly clean, dust-free conditions before being launched to Pluto in 2006.

EXPLORING SPACE

216 A spacecraft must be able to cope with the conditions in space and on other worlds. It is incredibly cold in space, but planets such as Venus are hotter than boiling water. Other planets have hazards such as clouds made of tiny drops of acid.

▶ The spacecraft *Galileo* was tested in ultra-bright light of the same level that it would receive as it flew nearer the Sun in 1990 on its way to Jupiter.

217 A robot submarine called *Endurance* may one day explore oceans on distant planets or moons. It has been tested in frozen lakes in Antarctica and near-boiling pools in New Zealand.

218 A test version of the spacecraft is tried on Earth. If successful, the real craft is built in strict conditions. One loose screw or speck of dust could cause disaster. There's no second chance once the mission begins.

93

Blast-off!

219 A spacecraft is blasted into space by its launch vehicle, or rocket. The rocket is the only machine powerful enough to reach "escape velocity"—the speed needed to break free from the pull of Earth's gravity. Usually the spacecraft is folded up in the nose cone of the rocket.

220 Different sizes of rockets are used for different sizes of spacecraft. One of the heaviest was the *Cassini-Huygens* mission to Saturn. At its launch in 1997, with all its fuel and equipment on board, it weighed 6 tons—about as much as a school bus. It needed a huge *Titan IV* rocket launcher to power it into space.

221 Spacecraft and other objects carried by the rocket are called the "payload." Most rockets take their payload into orbit around the Earth. The nose cone opens to release the craft stored inside. Parts of it unfold, such as the solar panels that turn sunlight into electricity.

◀ Launch vehicles must quickly reach escape velocity—36,750 feet per second—to shrug off Earth's gravitational pull.

Launch point
Escape velocity
Orbit bound by Earth's gravity

SECOND STAGE (S-II)
The middle section of the launcher had five J-2 rocket engines. It was 82 feet tall, and like the first stage, was 33 feet wide.

FIRST STAGE (S-IC)
The bottom part of *Saturn V* was 138 feet tall. The F-1 rocket engines propelled the entire launch vehicle for the first 37 miles.

J-2 rocket engines

F-1 rocket engines

▲ The biggest launchers were the three-stage *Saturn V* rockets used to launch the Apollo missions. Each stage fell away after using up its fuel.

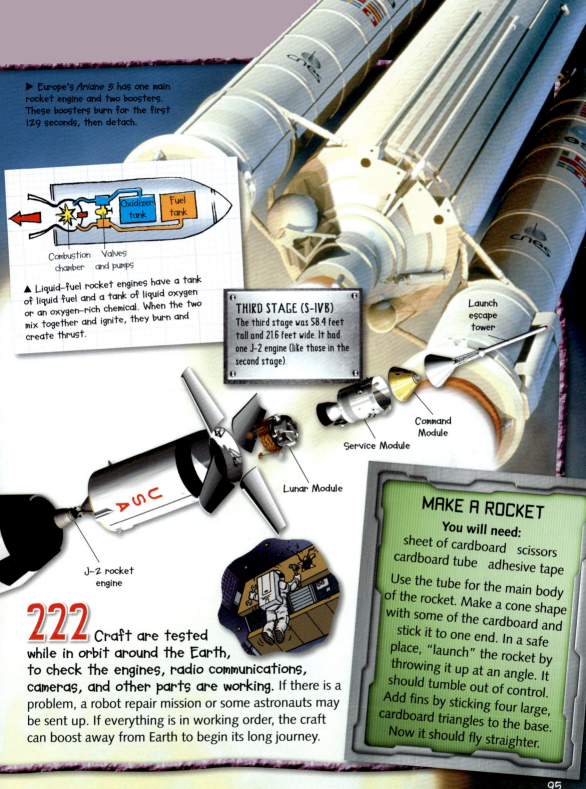

▶ Europe's *Ariane 5* has one main rocket engine and two boosters. These boosters burn for the first 129 seconds, then detach.

▲ Liquid-fuel rocket engines have a tank of liquid fuel and a tank of liquid oxygen or an oxygen-rich chemical. When the two mix together and ignite, they burn and create thrust.

THIRD STAGE (S-IVB)
The third stage was 58.4 feet tall and 21.6 feet wide. It had one J-2 engine (like those in the second stage).

222 Craft are tested while in orbit around the Earth, to check the engines, radio communications, cameras, and other parts are working. If there is a problem, a robot repair mission or some astronauts may be sent up. If everything is in working order, the craft can boost away from Earth to begin its long journey.

MAKE A ROCKET
You will need:
sheet of cardboard   scissors
cardboard tube   adhesive tape

Use the tube for the main body of the rocket. Make a cone shape with some of the cardboard and stick it to one end. In a safe place, "launch" the rocket by throwing it up at an angle. It should tumble out of control. Add fins by sticking four large, cardboard triangles to the base. Now it should fly straighter.

In deep space

223 Most spacecraft travel for months, even years, to their destinations. The fastest journey to Mars took just over six months, by *Mars Express* in 2003. *Pioneer 10* took 11 years to reach Neptune in 1983.

224 Launched in 2001, spacecraft *Deep Space 1* went on a trip to visit asteroids and comets. Its fuel tank was the size of a small suitcase, yet the fuel lasted for over three years.

◄ *Mars Express* cruised at a speed of 6,710 miles an hour on its way to Mars.

225 Guiding the craft on its course is vital. A tiny error could mean that it misses its distant target by millions of miles. Mission controllers on Earth regularly check the craft's position with radio signals using the Deep Space Network (DSN). The DSN is made up of three huge radio dishes located in California, Madrid in Spain, and Canberra, Australia.

▼ This ion thruster is being tested in a vacuum chamber. The blue glow is the beam of charged atoms being thrown out of the engine.

226 Spacecraft only need small engines because there is no air in space to slow them down. Depending on the length of the journey, different kinds of engines and fuels are used. Ion thrusters use magnetism made by electricity—hurling tiny particles, called ions, backward, to push the craft forward.

◀ Bowl-shaped antennae (aerials), like *New Horizons*', exchange radio signals to and from Earth.

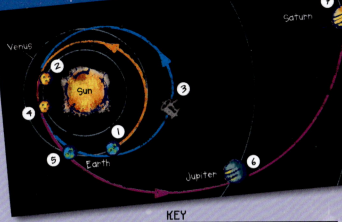
▲ *Cassini-Huygens*' journey to Saturn involved four gravity-assists. The main stages were: launch to first Venus flyby (orange), second Venus flyby (blue), and Earth flyby, past Jupiter to Saturn (purple).

KEY
1. October 1997 Launch from Earth
2. April 1998 First Venus flyby
3. December 1998 Engine fires for 90 minutes to return to Venus
4. June 1999 Second Venus flyby
5. August 1999 Earth-Moon flyby
6. December 2000 Jupiter flyby
7. July 2004 Arrives in orbit around Saturn

227 Craft often pass other planets or moons on their journeys. Like Earth, these objects all have a gravitational pull, and this could send a craft off course. However, a planet's gravity may be used to propel the craft in a new direction to save fuel. This is known as a gravity-assisted flyby or "slingshot."

◀▼ The three Deep Space Network sites are equally spaced around Earth, with 120 degrees between them, making a 360-degree circle.

The Deep Space Network's radio dish at Goldstone near Barstow, California, is 230 feet across.

228 For long periods, much of a craft's equipment shuts down to save electricity. It's like an animal hibernating in winter or a cell phone on stand-by. When the craft "hibernates" only a few vital systems stay active, such as navigation.

Ready to explore

229 As the spacecraft approaches its target, its systems power up and it "comes to life." Controllers on Earth test the craft's radio communications and other equipment. At such enormous distances, radio signals can take minutes, even hours, to make the journey.

230 Among the most important devices onboard a craft are cameras. Some work like telescopes to take a close-up or magnified view of a small area. Others are wide-angle cameras, which capture a much greater area without magnifying.

231 Other kinds of camera can "see" types of waves that are invisible to the human eye. These include infrared or heat rays, ultraviolet rays, radio waves, and X-rays. These rays and waves provide information about the target world, such as how hot or cold it is.

▼ *Mars Reconnaissance Orbiter*'s photograph of the 2,395-feet-wide Victoria Crater was captured by its high-resolution camera and shows amazing detail.

The Mars Climate Sounder records the temperature, moisture, and dust in the Martian atmosphere.

The high-resolution camera captures close-up, detailed photographs of the surface.

QUIZ

Spacecraft have many devices, but rarely microphones to detect sound. Why?

A. The chance of meeting aliens who can shout loudly is very small.
B. Sound waves do not travel through the vacuum of space.
C. It's too difficult to change sound waves into radio signals.

Answer: B

EXPLORING SPACE

232 **Magnetometers detect magnetic fields, which exist naturally around some planets, including Earth.** Gravitometers measure the target object's pull of gravity. This is especially important in the final stage of the journey—the landing. Some spacecraft also have space dust collectors.

Antenna

Solar panel

◀ *Mars Reconnaissance Orbiter*, launched in 2005, carries a telescopic camera, wide-angle cameras, sensors for infrared and ultraviolet light, and a radar that "sees" below the surface.

The spectrometer identifies different substances on the surface by measuring how much light is reflected.

The sub-surface radar can see up to 0.6 miles below the planet's surface.

233 **The information from the cameras and sensors is turned into radio signal codes and beamed back to Earth.** To send and receive these signals, the craft has one or more dish-shaped antennae. These must be in the correct position to communicate with the dishes located on Earth.

Flyby, bye-bye

234 On a flyby mission, a spacecraft comes close to its target. It does not go into orbit around it or land—it flies onward and away into deep space. Some flybys are part of longer missions to even more distant destinations. In these cases the flyby may also involve gravity assist.

LAUNCH FROM EARTH
August 20, 1977

235 A flyby craft may pass its target several times on a long, lop-sided path, before leaving again. Each pass gives a different view of the target object. The craft's cameras, sensors, and other equipment switch on to take pictures and record measurements, then turn off again as it flies away.

JUPITER

Flyby on July 9, 1979

236 The ultimate flyby craft was *Voyager 2*. It made a "Grand Tour" of the four outermost planets, which are only suitably aligned every 175 years. *Voyager 2* blasted off in 1977 and flew past Jupiter in 1979, Saturn in 1981, Uranus in 1986, and Neptune in 1989. This craft is still sending back information from a distance twice as far as Pluto is from Earth.

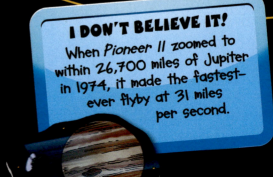

I DON'T BELIEVE IT!
When *Pioneer 11* zoomed to within 26,700 miles of Jupiter in 1974, it made the fastest-ever flyby at 31 miles per second.

◄ Voyager 2's golden disk (like an old vinyl record) is attached to its main body. The disk contains sounds and pictures from Earth for any aliens that may find it.

NEPTUNE

Flyby on August 25, 1989

URANUS

Flyby on January 24, 1986

► Voyager 2 made the greatest-ever tour of the Solar System. It is still the only spacecraft to fly close to Uranus and Neptune.

▼ A heat photograph taken from a distance of 3,000 miles shows Borrelly's tail trailing behind.

SATURN

Flyby on August 25, 1981

237 In 2001, after visiting the asteroid Braille, *Deep Space 1* flew past Comet Borrelly at 10 miles per second! At its closest, the craft was just 1,349 miles from the comet's solid center, which is as big as Mount Everest. *Deep Space 1*'s cameras took over 30 pictures before the craft was shut down.

▲ The main body of *Deep Space 1* was about the size of a large double bed.

Into orbit

238 On many exploring missions the craft is designed to go into orbit around its target world. Craft that do this are called orbiters, and they provide a much longer, closer look than a flyby mission.

▶ There are several different types of orbit that craft can make around their targets. Here, they are shown around Earth.

A polar orbit passes over the North and South Poles.

An equatorial orbit goes around the middle (Equator).

Most orbits are elliptical, with low and high points.

239 One of the most elliptical orbits was made by *Mars Global Surveyor*. At its closest, it passed Mars at a distance of 106 miles, twice in each orbit. The craft's furthest distance away was more than ten times greater.

◀ In 2006, two twin STEREO-craft went into orbit around the Sun. With one in front and one behind Earth, the craft made the first 3D observations of the Sun.

Antenna

ORBITER

You will need:
sock   tennis ball   string (3 feet long)

Put the ball in the sock and tie up the top with the string. Go outside. Holding the string half way along its length, whirl the sock above your head so that it "orbits" you. Gradually lengthen the string—does the "orbit" take longer?

DIONE

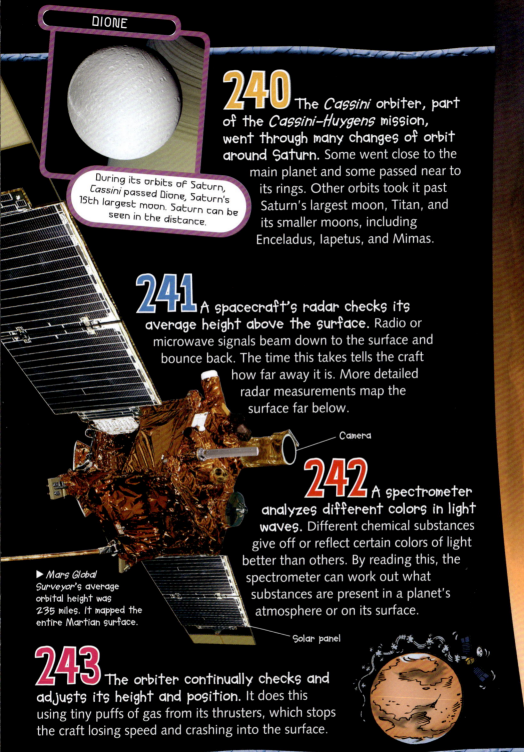

During its orbits of Saturn, Cassini passed Dione, Saturn's 15th largest moon. Saturn can be seen in the distance.

240 The *Cassini* orbiter, part of the *Cassini-Huygens* mission, went through many changes of orbit around Saturn. Some went close to the main planet and some passed near to its rings. Other orbits took it past Saturn's largest moon, Titan, and its smaller moons, including Enceladus, Iapetus, and Mimas.

241 A spacecraft's radar checks its average height above the surface. Radio or microwave signals beam down to the surface and bounce back. The time this takes tells the craft how far away it is. More detailed radar measurements map the surface far below.

Camera

242 A spectrometer analyzes different colors in light waves. Different chemical substances give off or reflect certain colors of light better than others. By reading this, the spectrometer can work out what substances are present in a planet's atmosphere or on its surface.

▶ *Mars Global Surveyor's* average orbital height was 235 miles. It mapped the entire Martian surface.

Solar panel

243 The orbiter continually checks and adjusts its height and position. It does this using tiny puffs of gas from its thrusters, which stops the craft losing speed and crashing into the surface.

Landers and impactors

244 Some missions have landers that touch down onto the surface of their target world. Part of the spacecraft may detach and land while the other part stays in orbit, or the whole spacecraft may land.

▶ The later landers of the Russian *Venera* program (1961–1983) used parachutes to slow down in the thick, hot, cloudy atmosphere of Venus.

① Spacecraft in orbit.

② Landing module separates from orbiter.

③ First parachute opened, then detached.

④ Main parachutes opened at a height of 30 miles above the surface.

⑤ Ring-shaped shock absorber filled with compressed gas lessened the impact at touchdown.

245 The journey down can be hazardous. If the planet has an atmosphere (layer of gas around it) there may be strong winds that could blow the lander off course. If the atmosphere is thick, there may be huge pressure pushing on the craft.

246 If there is an atmosphere, the lander may use parachutes, or inflate its own balloons or air bags, to slow its speed. On the *Cassini-Huygens* mission, the *Huygens* lander used two parachutes as it descended for touchdown on Saturn's moon, Titan.

247 If there is no atmosphere, retro-thrusters are used to slow the craft down. These puff gases in the direction of travel. Most landers have a strong, bouncy casing for protection as they hit the surface, or long, springy legs to reduce the impact.

▲ This image shows how *Beagle 2*'s solar panels were designed to fold out. However contact with the lander was lost soon after it detached from its orbiter in 2003.

▲ A photograph taken by *Deep Impact* 67 seconds after its impactor crashed into Comet Tempel 1, shows material being thrown out.

248 **After touchdown, the lander's solar panels and other parts fold out.** Its equipment and systems switch on, and it tests its radio communications with the orbiter and sometimes directly with Earth.

Impactor

249 **Some craft are designed to smash into their target, and these are called impactors.** The crash is observed by the orbiter and may also be watched by controllers on Earth. The dust, rocks, and gases given off by an impact provide valuable information about the target object.

Camera

▶ In 2005, *Deep Impact* released its impactor, watched it strike Comet Tempel 1, and studied the resulting crater.

◀ *Mars Pathfinder* lander being tested on Earth. It used a parachute, retro-thrusters, and multi-bubble air bags to land on Mars.

Robotic rovers

250 After touchdown, some landers release small, robotic vehicles called rovers. They have wheels and motors so they can move around on the surface to explore. So far rovers have explored on the Moon and Mars.

▶ In the 1970s, Russia sent two rovers, *Lunokhod* 1 and 2, to the Moon. Each was the size of a large bathtub, weighed around one ton and had eight wheels driven by electric motors.

Labels: Antennae, Laser reflector, Solar panels, Cameras, Wheels

QUIZ

How were the Mars rovers *Spirit* and *Opportunity* named?
1. Words chosen at random.
2. By a group of space experts.
3. By a 9-year-old girl, who won a competition.

Answer:
3. Siberian-born American schoolgirl Sofi Collis won the 2003 "Name the Rovers" competition

251 Modern rovers are mostly robotic— self-controlled using onboard computers. This is because of the time delay of radio signals. Even when Earth and Mars are at their closest distance to each other, radio signals take over three minutes to travel one way. If a rover was driven by remote control from Earth, it could have fallen off a cliff long before its onboard cameras relayed images of this.

252 **Rovers are designed and tested to survive the conditions on their target world.** Scientists know about these conditions from information collected from observations on Earth, and from previous missions. Test rovers are driven on extreme landscapes on Earth to make sure they can handle tricky terrain.

▲ A test version of a new rover destined for Mars, here being tested on the slippery rocks of a beach in Wales, U.K.

253 **The *Spirit* and *Opportunity* rovers landed on Mars in 2004.** They were equipped with cameras that allowed them to navigate around obstacles. Heat-sensitive cameras detected levels of heat soaked up by rocks, giving clues to what the rocks are made of. Onboard microscopes and magnets gathered and studied dust particles containing iron.

▶ Twin rovers *Spirit* and *Opportunity* were each about the size of an office desk.

Navcam.
Antenna.
Main antenna.
Solar panels.
Mobile arm carried five gadgets including a camera, rock grinder, and magnets.
Each wheel had an electric motor.

254 **A rover for Venus is planned, but its surface temperature is over 750°F.** Plastics and some metals would melt there. A Venus rover would have to be made out of metals, such as titanium, which have high melting points. Its inner workings would need to be continually cooled.

107

Close-up look

▶ In the late 1970s the U.S.'s two Viking landers photographed their robotic sampler arms digging into Mars' surface.

255 Some landers and rovers have robot arms that extend from the main body. These scoop or drill into the surface to collect samples, which are then tested in the craft's onboard science laboratory. Samples are tested for chemical reactions, such as bubbling or changing color.

Solar panel.

Robotic arm with scoop and camera.

Spheres of minerals containing iron, known as "blueberries."

Circular area ground by tool is 1.8 inches across.

256 Most rovers have six wheels. This design allows them to move quickly around sharp corners, without tipping over. Each wheel has an electric motor, powered by onboard batteries that are charged by the solar panels. If the batteries run down, the rover "sleeps" until light from the Sun recharges them.

◀ Mars rovers *Spirit* and *Opportunity* were both equipped with a rock-grinding tool. They used it to grind into rocks and gather dust samples.

EXPLORING SPACE

257 The *Phoenix* Mars lander had several devices on its robotic arm to measure features of Martian soil. It measured how easily it carried (conducted) heat and electricity, and if it contained any liquids. *Phoenix* also had microscopes for an ultra-close view of the surface samples.

258 One type of rover drill uses heat to melt or burn a hole, which could be useful on icy planets. A thermal rover could even melt its way through ice, perhaps to water beneath, to look for alien life.

259 Most landers and rovers have mini weather stations. Sensors measure temperatures and pressures through the day and night and record the Sun's brightness. They also take samples of gases if there is an atmosphere, and record weather, such as wind and dust storms.

Meteorological (weather) station.
Gas analyzers.
Mini science laboratory.
Solar panel.

◀ The *Phoenix* Mars lander of 2008 had a robotic arm, on the left, and a small weather station.

260 The orbiting craft acts as a relay station to receive signals from its lander and send them on to Earth. A lander can, in turn, be a relay station for a rover. A rover has a small radio set to communicate with the lander and the lander has a slightly larger one to communicate with the orbiter. The orbiter has the biggest radio set to communicate with Earth.

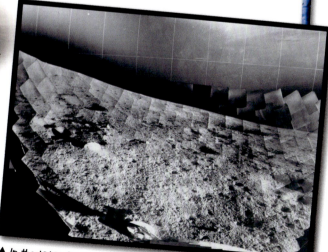

▲ In the 1960s five U.S. Surveyor landers sent back close-up photographs of the Moon's surface. These were joined together to make larger scenes.

109

Exploring Mars

JUL 1965 *Mariner 4* flew past Mars and took the first close-up photos of another planet.

NOV 1971 *Mariner 9* entered orbit around Mars—the first craft to orbit another planet.

261 Mars is the nearest planet to Earth and the most explored. In the 1870s, astronomers thought they could see canals of water on Mars' surface, thought to be built by aliens. But with better telescopes, these "canals" were found to be simply a trick of the light.

▼ This timeline shows some of the most notable missions in the exploration of Mars.

DEC 1971 *Mars 3*'s lander was the first to touch down safely on Mars, but contact was lost after 20 seconds.

262 Since the 1960s more than 40 missions have set off to Mars. About two thirds of them failed at launch or on the way. One quarter have failed at or near Mars, leading some people to believe that Martians were attacking and destroying the craft.

JUL/SEP 1976 *Viking 1* and *2* were the first successful landers on the surface of Mars.

JUL 1997 *Mars Pathfinder* landed and released *Sojourner*, the first rover on another planet.

◀ *Mars Odyssey* (2001) produced this image of Mars' south pole. The Martian polar ice caps are made of frozen water and "dry ice"—solid (frozen) carbon dioxide.

263 In 1976, two U.S. Viking landers carried out research on Mars. They took many photographs, made detailed maps, and tested the atmosphere, rocks, and soil, but they found no definite signs of life. In 2008, the U.S. *Phoenix* lander discovered water frozen as ice, and many minerals and chemicals in the soil.

264 The *Spirit* and *Opportunity* rovers made an amazing series of explorations and discoveries. They found evidence that there was once water on Mars, and that it is possibly still there underground. In 2009 *Spirit* got stuck in soft soil but *Opportunity* continued until 2018.

MAY 2008 *Phoenix* lander touched down. It was the first craft to land in Mars' polar area.

SEP 1997 *Mars Global Surveyor* went into orbit and began detailed, large-scale mapping of the surface.

DEC 2003 In orbit, *Mars Express* released its lander, *Beagle 2*, but communications to it were lost.

MAR 2006 *Mars Reconnaissance Orbiter* arrived, making a record six working craft in orbit or on the surface of Mars.

JAN 2004 *Mars Exploration Rovers Spirit* and *Opportunity* arrived on the surface, ready to explore.

265 The *Mars Science Laboratory* rover *Curiosity* landed in 2012. In 2021, the *Perseverance* rover arrived, landing at the site of an ancient lakebed. Both rovers have a drill, sampling arm, and scientific tools to search for signs of past life on Mars.

◀ *Curiosity* is about the size of a Mini car and has a top speed of one inch per second.

Back on Earth

266 All spacecraft have a mission control center on Earth. Expert teams monitor a craft's systems, including radio communications, and the data a craft collects from its cameras and instruments.

▲ Mission controllers at NASA's Jet Propulsion Laboratory in California celebrate as the first images from rover Opportunity reach Earth.

267 Missions often run into problems. Controllers must work out how to keep a mission going when faults occur. If power supplies fail, the teams may have to decide to switch off some equipment so that others can continue working.

268 Sample return missions bring items from space back to Earth. In 2004, the *Genesis* craft dropped off its return container. It was supposed to parachute down to Earth's surface, but it crash-landed in Utah. Luckily, some of its samples of solar wind survived for study.

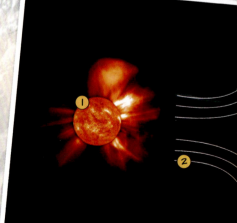

269 Gases, dust, rocks, and other items are brought back to Earth to be studied. In the early 1970s the six manned Apollo missions brought a total of 841.5 pounds of Moon material back to Earth.

▲ This piece of basalt Moon rock, brought back by *Apollo 15*, is being studied by *Apollo 17* astronaut and geologist (rock expert) Jack Schmitt.

270 Samples returned from space must not be contaminated with material from Earth. Keeping samples clean allows scientists to find out what they contain, and stops any dangerous substances being released on Earth. Spacecraft are ultra-clean at launch to prevent them spreading chemicals or germs from Earth to other worlds.

▼ *Genesis* collected high-energy particles from the Sun's solar wind, which distorts Earth's magnetic field.

I DON'T BELIEVE IT!
Moon rocks don't look very special, yet over 100 small ones brought back by the Apollo missions have been stolen. More than ten people have been caught trying to sell them.

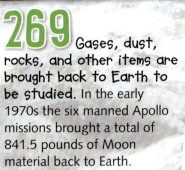

▶ This sample of Moon rock collected during the *Apollo 11* mission is housed inside a securely fastened, airtight container.

KEY
1. Sun
2. Solar wind
3. Bow shock (where the solar wind meets Earth's magnetic field)
4. Earth's magnetic field
5. Earth

Toward the Sun

◀ This photograph taken by *SOHO* uses a disk with a hole to block out some of the Sun's glare. This reveals vast streaming clouds of superheated matter called plasma.

Corona

Coronal mass ejection (CME) of superheated plasma

271 **Missions to the Sun encounter enormous heat.** In the 1970s the U.S.-German craft *Helios 2* flew to within 27 million miles of the Sun. From 1990, the *Ulysses* probe traveled on a huge orbit, passing near the Sun and as far out as Jupiter.

272 **In 1996, the *SOHO* spacecraft began studying the Sun from near Earth.** Since then, it has found many new comets. The *Parker Solar Probe* is now orbiting the Sun, and at its closest point will fly to 4 million miles from the surface. It has a shield of heat-resistant material for protection.

◀ The Helios mission was featured on stamps worldwide.

EXPLORING SPACE

▲ *Messenger* had a "sunshade" made out of a ceramic-composite material to protect it from the Sun's heat.

274 Mercury, the nearest planet to the Sun, has been visited by two spacecraft, *Mariner 10* in 1974, and *Messenger* in 2004. *Messenger* made flybys in 2008 and 2009 and went into orbit in 2011. These craft measured Mercury's surface temperature at 790°F—twice as hot as a home oven.

273 Missions to Venus include Russia's Venera series (1961 to 1984), U.S. Mariner probes (1962 to 1973) and *Pioneer Venus* (1978). From 1990 to 1994, *Magellan* used radar to map the surface in amazing detail. In 2006, Europe's *Venus Express* began more mapping. Its instruments also studied Venus' extreme global warming.

275 More than 20 craft have visited Venus, the second planet from the Sun. Its atmosphere of thick clouds, extreme pressures, temperatures over 840°F, and acid chemicals, pose huge challenges for exploring craft.

Antenna
Solar panel
Positioning thrusters
Main rocket engine
Gold coating helps to keep out the Sun's heat.

◀ Studying Venus' atmosphere may help us understand similar climate processes happening on Earth.

▲ *Venus Express* orbited as low as 155 miles above the poles of Venus.

276 The *Parker Solar Probe* is the fastest spacecraft ever. In April 2021 it neared the Sun at 93 miles per second!

Asteroids near and far

277 **Asteroids orbit the Sun but are far smaller than planets, so even finding them is a challenge.** Most large asteroids are in the main asteroid belt between Mars and Jupiter. Much closer to us are near-Earth Asteroids (NEAs), and more than 20 have been explored in detail by flyby craft, orbiters, and landers.

278 **Orbiting and landing on asteroids is very difficult.** Many asteroids are oddly shaped, and they roll and tumble as they move through space. A craft may only discover this as it gets close.

◀ Dwarf planet Ceres and the three largest asteroids in our Solar System, seen against North America for scale. Vesta, the biggest asteroid, is about 330 miles across.

279 **In 1996, the probe NEAR-Shoemaker launched toward NEA Eros.** On the way it flew past asteroid Mathilde in the main belt. Then in 2000 it orbited 21-mile-long Eros, before landing. The probe discovered that the asteroid was peanut-shaped, and also gathered information about Eros' rocks, magnetism, and movement. In 2008, spacecraft *Rosetta* passed main belt asteroid Steins, and asteroid Lutetia in 2010.

EXPLORING SPACE

Jupiter

▲ In the main belt there are some dense "asteroid swarms." But most larger asteroids are thousands of miles apart.

280 In 2010 Japan's *Hayabusa* brought back samples of asteroid Itokawa after touching down on its surface in 2005. This information has helped our understanding of asteroids as "leftovers" from the formation of the Solar System 4,600 million years ago.

281 The *Dawn* spacecraft was launched in 2007. It explored Vesta—the biggest asteroid—in 2011–2012 and went into orbit around the dwarf planet Ceres in 2015. It investigated features of the two asteroids and what their surfaces are made of.

▶ *Hayabusa* was designed to gather samples of the asteroid Itokawa by firing a metal pellet toward the surface. It could then collect the dust thrown up by the impact.

▲ The *Dawn* mission badge shows its two main targets.

Comet mysteries

282 Comets travel to and from the edges of the Solar System and beyond as they orbit the Sun. Unlike long-period comets, which may take thousands of years to orbit, short-period comets orbit every 200 years or less and so can be explored.

▶ The Oort cloud surrounds the Solar System and is made up of icy objects. It may be the source of some Sun-orbiting comets.

▶ The Kuiper belt lies beyond Neptune's orbit and is about twice the size of the Solar System. It consists of lots of cometlike objects.

283 Like asteroids, comets are difficult to find. Comets warm up and glow only as they near the Sun. Their tails are millions of miles long, but consist only of faint gases and dust. The center, or nucleus, of a comet may give off powerful jets of dust and gases that could blow a craft off course.

▶ A typical comet is mostly dust and ice. It has a glowing area, or coma, around it, and a long tail that points away from the Sun.

Solid rock core.
Nucleus is often only a few miles across.
Jets of gas and dust escape as ice melts.
Glowing cloud, or coma, around nucleus is illuminated by sunlight.
Dust and ice surrounds core.

EXPLORING SPACE

284 The famous Halley's Comet last appeared in 1986. Several exploring craft, known as the "Halley Armada," went to visit it. This included Europe's *Giotto* probe, which flew to within 400 miles of the comet's nucleus. There were also two Russian-French Vega probes, and *Sakigake* and *Suisei* from Japan.

DUST COLLECTED FROM COMET WILD 2

Comet dust particles

▲ Under the microscope, a piece of *Stardust*'s aerogel (half the size of this "o") is revealed to have minute dust particles embedded within it.

▶ *Stardust* collected comet dust using a very lightweight foam, called aerogel, in a collector shaped like a tennis racket. The collector folded into the craft's bowl-like capsule for return to Earth.

285 In 2008, the *Stardust* probe returned a capsule of dust collected from the comet Wild 2. In 2005, *Deep Impact* visited Comet Tempel 1 and released an impactor to crash into its nucleus and study the dust and gases given off. These craft increase our knowledge of comets as frozen balls of icy chemicals, rock, and dust.

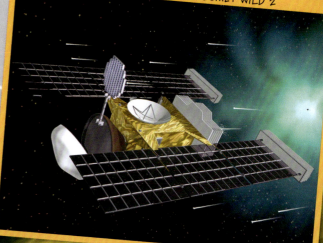

STARDUST APPROACHING COMET WILD 2

Glowing dust tail illuminated by sunlight.

Ion (gas) tail appears bluish.

SAMPLE CAPSULE RETURNS TO EARTH

Gas giants

286 The four furthest planets from Earth—Jupiter, Saturn, Uranus, and Neptune—are "gas giants." These are large planets composed mainly of gases. It takes at least two years to reach Jupiter by the most direct route. But craft usually take longer because they use gravity assist.

▼ *Galileo* orbited Jupiter for more than seven years. It released an atmosphere probe to study the gases that make up almost the whole planet.

287 Craft entering Neptune's atmosphere would be hit by the fastest winds in the Solar System. These are ten times stronger than a hurricane on Earth!

288 There have been seven flybys of Jupiter and each one discovered more of the planet's moons. The two U.S. Voyager missions, launched in 1977, discovered that Jupiter has rings like Saturn. U.S. spacecraft *Galileo* arrived in orbit around Jupiter in 1995 and released a probe into the planet's atmosphere.

EXPLORING SPACE

▲ *Huygens'* pictures from the surface of Titan, Saturn's largest moon, show lumps of ice and a haze of deadly methane gas.

ON TITAN'S SURFACE

289 The ringed planet Saturn had flybys by *Pioneer 11* (1979) and *Voyagers 1* and *2* (1980–1981). In 2004 the huge *Cassini-Huygens* craft arrived after a seven-year journey. The orbiter *Cassini* took spectacular photographs of the planet, its rings, and its moons.

▼ The *Huygens* lander separated from *Cassini* and headed for Titan. It sent back more than 750 images from the surface.

TITAN

A heat shield prevented burn-up on entry.

Parachutes slowed the lander's descent.

Huygens lands on Titan.

290 The only exploring craft to have visited Uranus and Neptune is *Voyager 2*. During its flyby of Uranus in 1986, *Voyager 2* discovered ten new moons and two new rings. In 1989, the craft passed the outermost planet, Neptune, and discovered six new moons and four new rings.

▼ The four gas giants have many moons—some large, and some very small. This list includes the five largest moons for each (not to scale).

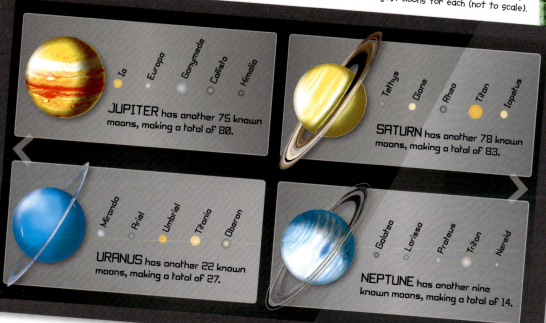

JUPITER has another 75 known moons, making a total of 80. (Io, Europa, Ganymede, Callisto, Himalia)

SATURN has another 78 known moons, making a total of 83. (Tethys, Dione, Rhea, Titan, Iapetus)

URANUS has another 22 known moons, making a total of 27. (Miranda, Ariel, Umbriel, Titania, Oberon)

NEPTUNE has another nine known moons, making a total of 14. (Galatea, Larissa, Proteus, Triton, Nereid)

SPACE TRAVEL

291 The vast distances in space make it extremely difficult to travel to even the closest planets. The furthest humans have ever been is to the Moon, and it took three days to get there. It would take months to get to the nearest planets, and thousands of years to reach the closest star.

◀ Astronauts can now live in space, in the orbiting International Space Station, seen here reflected in the visor of NASA astronaut Mike Hopkins' spacesuit.

Escape from Earth

292 Gravity is the force that pulls everything down toward Earth. All objects are pulled toward each other by gravity, but bigger things have a stronger pull. Earth is huge, and so pulls everything smaller toward it. This is why you don't float away, and why it is difficult to travel into space.

Fast car (70 miles an hour)

Jet airliner (560 miles an hour)

Spacecraft (17,000 miles an hour)

◀ A spacecraft traveling at less than 17,000 miles an hour will fall back to Earth, pulled down by gravity.

293 The way to overcome this pull of gravity and reach space is to travel very fast. A spacecraft must get up to a speed of about 17,000 miles an hour. This is about 30 times faster than a cruising jet airliner, and 250 times faster than a car traveling on an expressway.

294 Even 17,000 miles an hour is not fast enough for a spacecraft to break free of Earth's gravity. At this speed it will circle round Earth about 120 miles above the ground—it is in orbit. Spacecraft orbit at different speeds depending on their distance from Earth—the pull of gravity decreases the further you are from Earth.

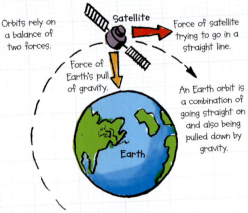

Orbits rely on a balance of two forces.

Satellite

Force of satellite trying to go in a straight line.

Force of Earth's pull of gravity.

An Earth orbit is a combination of going straight on and also being pulled down by gravity.

Earth

▲ Satellites orbiting closer to Earth must travel much faster than those in higher orbits.

SPACE TRAVEL

◀ An Atlas rocket gave the *New Horizons* space probe the fastest ever launch speed for its journey to distant Pluto.

295 **Spacecraft need even more speed to escape from the pull of Earth's gravity completely and fly off into space.** They have to travel at 25,000 miles an hour—this speed is called Earth's escape velocity. Once in space there is no air to slow a spacecraft down, so it doesn't need powerful engines to keep going.

QUIZ
1. How fast is Earth's escape velocity?
2. How far away is the nearest star from the Sun?
3. What is the name of the force that stops you just floating away from Earth?

Answers:
1. 25,000 miles an hour 2. 4.2 light-years (25 million million miles) 3. Gravity

296 **Distances in space are vast—so huge that astronomers do not use miles or kilometers to measure them.** One measure of distance is the light-year, which is the distance that light travels in one year, and is equal to 5.88 million million miles. The nearest star to the Sun is 4.2 light-years away—equivalent to nearly 25 million million miles.

Sun — Light takes 8 minutes to reach Earth from the Sun. — Earth

▲ A car traveling at 37 miles an hour would take 285 years to get to the Sun.

Rocket power

297 Rocket engines provide the enormous power needed to launch a spacecraft with enough speed to fly into space. On Earth, engines use oxygen from the air to burn their fuel, but in space there is no air to provide oxygen. Rocket engines can work in space because they have their own supply of oxygen gas.

298 Inside a rocket engine, fuel is burned to make hot gases. The gases shoot out of a nozzle at the back of the rocket, pushing it forward at high speed. Some rockets use a liquid fuel, which is pumped into the engine where it is mixed with oxygen and burned. Other rockets use solid fuel—a rubbery material containing oxygen.

KEY
1. Satellite payload
2. Second stage
3. First stage
4. Liquid oxygen tank
5. Liquid hydrogen fuel tank
6. Booster rocket
7. Solid fuel
8. First stage engine

▶ An Ariane 5 rocket has two stages and two solid rocket boosters to launch satellites into orbit.

299 **Booster rockets can supply extra power for a launch.** These are separate rockets strapped to the side of the main rocket. They burn their fuel then break away and fall back to Earth. The space shuttle used two huge booster rockets, and the Russian Soyuz rockets have four boosters strapped around them at take-off.

▶ Ariane 5 boosters burn their fuel in about two minutes then fall away into the sea.

▲ Ariane 5 launch: Lift-off (1), boosters fall away (2), first stage separates (3), second stage puts satellite into orbit (4).

MAKE A BALLOON ROCKET
You will need:
string   drinking straw   long balloon   sticky tape

Tie one end of the string to something solid and secure, like a doorknob. Thread the string through the drinking straw and tie the other end to something solid and secure about 20 feet away, so that the string is tight. Blow up the balloon and, while holding the neck, stick it to the straw with the sticky tape. Let go of the balloon and watch the straw fly along the string. The air escaping from the balloon pushes it along, like the fiery jet of burning gas from a rocket. The pushing force that moves the balloon and a real rocket is called thrust.

300 **Several rocket stages are needed to reach space.** Each stage has its own engine and fuel. The first stage lifts the rocket and spacecraft off the ground. When it has used up its fuel, it separates from the rest of the rocket and falls back to Earth. The next stage engine starts up, giving the rocket extra speed. It then falls away and the third stage takes the spacecraft into orbit.

301 **New spaceplanes are being designed that may make it easier and cheaper to fly into space.** One is called *Skylon*. It will have engines that can use oxygen gas from the air until it reaches space. This means it will be lighter and need less power to take off because it will carry less oxygen. *Skylon* will take off and land on a runway and will be able to fly many times.

Space shuttle

302 Most rockets can only be launched once, but the space shuttle was a reusable spaceplane with rocket engines. It had three main parts: an orbiter, a huge fuel tank, and two giant boosters. Only the orbiter went into space. Five orbiters were built—*Columbia*, *Challenger*, *Discovery*, *Atlantis*, and *Endeavour*—and each flew in space many times.

▶ At lift-off the enormous tank supplied the shuttle's three main engines with fuel. While the shuttle was attached to the tank during lift-off, its cargo bay doors were shut. The doors only opened when the shuttle reached orbit.

Empty booster weighs about 100 tons.
Booster rockets separate two minutes after launch.
Hubble telescope carried in cargo bay
Cargo bay door
Flight deck
Orbiter
Cargo bay
Main engines
Liquid fuel

303 The shuttle took off upward like a rocket. The orbiter's three rocket engines and two huge booster rockets all fired together at launch. The solid fuel in the boosters only took two minutes to burn up, then they fell away into the sea.

▼ Each of the five shuttle orbiters flew into space many times. In total there were 135 flights between 1981 and 2011.

🚀 Shuttle flights

Orbiter	First flight	Last flight	No. of flights
Columbia	April 12, 1981	Jan 16, 2003	28
Challenger	April 4, 1983	Jan 28, 1986	10
Discovery	Aug 30, 1984	Feb 24, 2011	39
Atlantis	Oct 3, 1985	July 8, 2011	33
Endeavour	May 7, 1992	May 16, 2011	25

SPACE TRAVEL

I DON'T BELIEVE IT!
At launch the shuttle weighed about 4.4 million pounds, but most of this was fuel. The fuel weighed about 20 times more than the orbiter, which weighed about the same as ten elephants.

Fuel tank

Double-skin tank walls

Boosters

304 The shuttle orbiter could carry seven astronauts into space. They lived and worked in the cabin at the front of the orbiter on missions lasting one to two weeks at a time.

305 Satellites were launched from the shuttle's cargo bay. The shuttle placed the Hubble Space Telescope into orbit, and there were five later shuttle missions to repair it in space. On other flights the cargo bay held a laboratory called Spacelab where the astronauts carried out experiments.

306 The shuttle orbiters carried many of the International Space Station's parts into space. Space station modules where the astronauts would live and work fitted into the shuttle's cargo bay for the journey. Each part was added to the space station by spacewalking astronauts, who gradually built it while it orbited Earth.

▼ Space shuttle *Atlantis* docked with the ISS during the shuttle's final mission in July 2011.

Returning to Earth

307 One of the most dangerous parts of space travel is reentry (returning to Earth's atmosphere). When spacecraft come back they rub against the air at incredible speeds, which makes them extremely hot. The space shuttle reached temperatures of about 3,000°F on reentry.

▲ The shuttle glowed red hot when reentering Earth's atmosphere. To avoid burning up, spacecraft must reenter at exactly the right angle.

308 Astronauts in a returning spacecraft are protected from the heat by a heat shield. On the space shuttle the heat shield was made of special tiles that covered the shuttle's underside. These stopped the heat from reaching the rest of the shuttle. Other spacecraft like the Russian Soyuz are protected by thick material that burns away but keeps the spacecraft cool.

▼ A Soyuz space capsule carrying three cosmonauts home from the *Mir* space station throws up dust as it lands in a desert area.

309 The shuttle landed on a runway like an aircraft, but without using its engines, more like a huge glider. It traveled halfway round the world to its landing site, gliding through the air and slowing down by turning left and right. It came to a stop on the runway by using parachutes and brakes on its landing wheels to slow it. After servicing, the orbiter could be launched into space again.

◀ The space shuttle needed a very long runway to land safely at the end of a mission.

310 The Soyuz spacecraft uses parachutes to slow it down as it falls through the air. Just before it hits the ground, small rocket motors fire to slow it even more and give it a soft landing. Some early spacecraft, like the Command Modules from the Apollo missions to the Moon, came down to Earth by parachute before splashing into the sea for a soft landing.

FEEL THE HEAT OF FRICTION

Rub your hands together or rub them against your legs. Do they start to feel warm? This is the way a spacecraft heats up when it rubs against the air. A force called friction makes the heat by trying to stop the rubbing movement. You can even start a fire using friction by rubbing two dry sticks together.

Spacecraft

311 Spacecraft are vehicles that travel to destinations in space. Some are built to carry people onboard, but these do not travel far from Earth. Unmanned spacecraft can travel much further. People have sent unmanned spacecraft to all the other planets orbiting the Sun, and some space probes and rovers have even landed on some of them. Several have flown beyond the furthest planet in our Solar System, out toward the distant stars.

▶ The *Galileo* space probe orbited the giant planet Jupiter and dropped a smaller probe into Jupiter's bright clouds.

312 With no air to push against, a spacecraft will keep going steadily through space. However, spacecraft have engines to change direction and keep them on course, and to slow them down when they get to their destination. The engines can also provide extra speed to make the journey quicker. The spacecraft must carry all the fuel its engines need for the whole journey.

313 All spacecraft need power to operate and to keep warm—it is extremely cold in space. Solar panels that change sunlight into electricity can provide enough power for spacecraft close to the Sun. Those that travel far away from the Sun often use nuclear power. The space shuttle had fuel cells that made electricity by turning oxygen and hydrogen into water.

SPACE TRAVEL

314 Spacecraft send back information and receive instructions from controllers on Earth using radio signals. As a spacecraft travels further away the radio signals get weaker. Probes going to distant planets need large dish-shaped antennae (aerials) to send and receive messages. Back on Earth, huge receivers collect the faint signals.

I DON'T BELIEVE IT!

UFOs (Unidentified Flying Objects) are objects in the sky that do not look like ordinary planes. Some people think that UFOs are alien spacecraft from other stars or planets visiting Earth, but there is no evidence for this.

315 Manned spacecraft must be able to keep the astronauts inside alive and well. They are built with a strong double outer layer to protect the crew from dangerous radiation and speeding space dust. They contain a supply of air to breathe and enough water and food for the whole journey. The temperature is kept comfortable using radiators to lose excess heat into space.

Astronauts

▲ Trainee astronauts float inside an aircraft as if they are in space.

316 People who travel in space are called astronauts. In Russia they are called cosmonauts and in China they are called taikonauts. Astronauts from many different countries have gone into space, most of them in Russian and U.S. spacecraft. So far, the only country other than Russia and the U.S. to have launched astronauts into space is China.

▶ ESA (European Space Agency) astronaut Jean-Francois Clervoy trains for spacewalks wearing a spacesuit underwater.

317 Astronauts need many months of training to get them ready for a spaceflight. They learn about the spacecraft they will be living and working in, and what to do in an emergency. Astronauts train in huge tanks of water to get used to the feeling of weightlessness and practice for spacewalks outside the spacecraft.

SPACE TRAVEL

QUIZ
1. What are Chinese astronauts called?
2. How long do astronauts exercise for each day?
3. Why do astronauts train in huge tanks of water?

Answers:
1. Taikonauts 2. About two hours 3. To get used to the feeling of weightlessness

318 It is essential for astronauts to be fit and healthy. Before they fly there are many medical checks to make sure they will not fall ill in space. In their spacecraft they exercise regularly, usually for about two hours a day by using an exercise bike, running on a treadmill or doing a space version of weightlifting. This helps to keep their muscles and bones strong.

319 Living in space for a long time can make your muscles weaker and your body slightly taller. When floating in a spacecraft, you do not use the muscles that normally keep you standing up. The bones that make up your spine aren't squashed together by gravity, and so they stretch apart. Astronauts soon return to normal back on Earth.

320 Astronauts have many different jobs in space. Some are trained as pilots to fly the spacecraft. Others go outside the spacecraft or space station, where they carry out spacewalks to install equipment or do repairs. Inside, they perform experiments to explore the effects of space travel.

KEY
1. Spine stretches, making astronauts taller.
2. Leg and back muscles weaken.
3. Leg and back bones get weaker and thinner.
4. Face becomes puffy.

▼ In space, gravity does not pull down on an astronaut's body.

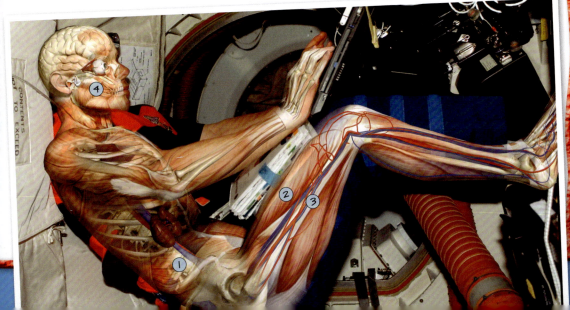

Space pioneers

321 The first person to fly into space was a Russian called Yuri Gagarin. On April 12, 1961 he completed one orbit round Earth in his spacecraft *Vostok 1*. Soon after Gagarin's flight, on May 5, 1961, Alan Shepard became the first American in space, although he didn't orbit Earth.

▲ Yuri Gagarin's historic flight lasted 1 hour and 48 minutes.

322 Two years after Gagarin's flight, on June 16, 1963, Valentina Tereshkova became the first woman in space. She spent nearly three days in orbit, circling Earth 48 times during her flight in the *Vostok 6* spacecraft.

▲ Valentina Tereshkova was only 26 when she flew in space.

323 The first person to leave a spacecraft and go on a spacewalk was a Russian called Alexei Leonov, on March 18, 1965. He was out in space for 12 minutes attached to his spacecraft by a tether to stop him floating away.

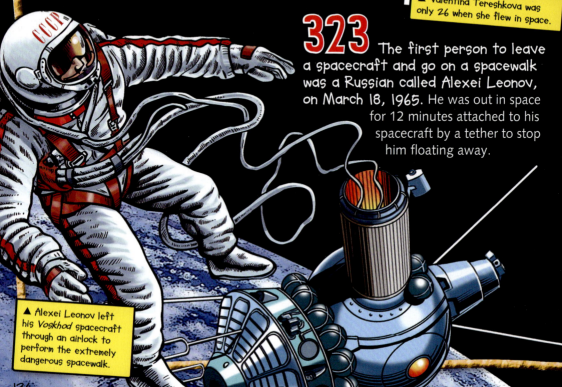

▲ Alexei Leonov left his *Voskhod* spacecraft through an airlock to perform the extremely dangerous spacewalk.

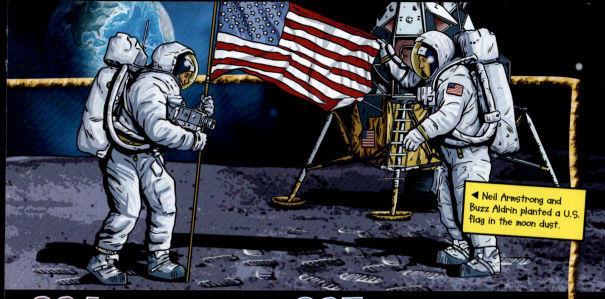

◀ Neil Armstrong and Buzz Aldrin planted a U.S. flag in the moon dust.

324 **The first Moon landing took place on July 20, 1969.** Two American astronauts landed the *Apollo 11* lunar lander in an area of the Moon called the Sea of Tranquility. Neil Armstrong was the first to set foot on the surface, followed by Buzz Aldrin. They spent about two and a half hours outside on the surface, exploring and collecting rocks to take back to Earth.

325 **Since these early pioneers, several astronauts have spent over a year in space.** Valeri Polyakov stayed aboard the *Mir* space station for nearly 438 days (about 14 months) in 1994 to 1995. Others have only spent longer in space if you add together all their different space flights. Gennady Padalka had five flights totalling 879 days (over two years).

SPACE TIMELINE

October 4, 1957
The first artificial satellite, Sputnik 1, was launched.

→ **November 3, 1957**
A dog called Laika became the first animal in space.

→ **April 12, 1961**
The first human, Yuri Gagarin, was launched into space.

July 20, 1969
The first manned spacecraft landed on the Moon, and Neil Armstrong became the first person to walk on the surface.

← **March 18, 1965**
Alexei Leonov was the first person to leave a spacecraft and "walk" in space.

← **June 16, 1963**
Valentina Tereshkova became the first woman in space.

April 19, 1971
The first space station, *Salyut 1*, was launched into orbit.

→ **December 14, 1972**
Apollo 17, the last manned mission to the Moon, left the Moon.

→ **April 12, 1981**
The first flight of the reuseable space shuttle.

→ **February 20, 1986**
The first module of the *Mir* space station was launched, with other modules and equipment added over the next 10 years.

October 31, 2000
The first crew visited the ISS.

← **November 20, 1998**
The first module of the International Space Station (ISS), Zarya, was launched.

← **March 22, 1995**
Valeri Polyakov set the record for the longest single spaceflight.

Spacesuits

326 Astronauts could not survive outside their spacecraft without a spacesuit. They put it on inside an airlock (airtight chamber) which has two doors, one opening into the spacecraft and the other to the outside. Once inside their suit they close the inner door, let the air out of the airlock, open the outer door and go outside.

327 Spacesuits are very bulky because they have to keep astronauts alive and protect them from speeding space dust. They are made of many different layers of material—14 for a NASA spacesuit. The outer layers are waterproof, fireproof, and bulletproof. Underneath are insulating layers that keep the temperature steady and a rip-proof layer that stops the suit from tearing.

328 The spacesuit must press down on an astronaut's body. Without this pressure their bodies would swell and gases would bubble out of their blood like boiling water. On Earth the air is always pressing down on our bodies, but in space there is no air. In a spacesuit the pressure comes from a double layer blown up like a balloon, in the shape of a human body.

KEY
1. Lights
2. Helmet
3. Visor
4. Gloves
5. Control panel
6. Tether
7. Backpack with life support system
8. Boots

▲ Spacesuits provide a life-support system for astronauts while outside the spacecraft.

SPACE TRAVEL

329 **Astronauts wear special underwear under their spacesuits to keep them cool.** The stretchy material fits closely, covering the whole body. Over 295 feet of thin tubing zig-zags through it. Cool water runs through these tubes, carrying heat away from the skin to the spacesuit backpack. Here the heat radiates out into space, cooling the water before it circulates through the tubes again.

330 **Spacesuits have several different parts that all fit together with airtight seals.** There are flexible joints in the shoulders, arms, and wrists so that the astronauts can move their hands and arms to work in space. The helmet over the head is made of tough clear plastic to give the astronaut a good view. Under the helmet, a cap with a radio lets the astronaut talk to other astronauts or ground control.

I DON'T BELIEVE IT!

The NASA spacesuits that the astronauts wear on spacewalks at the ISS cost $12 million each. Astronauts do not have their own individual spacesuits. The parts come in different sizes so each astronaut can put together a spacesuit that fits him or her.

Spacewalks

331 Extravehicular Activity (EVA), often called a spacewalk, is when an astronaut leaves the spacecraft to work outside in space. They might be building or repairing a space station, or servicing satellites. Experiments that need to be exposed directly to space are fixed to the outside of a spacecraft and collected during spacewalks.

◀ This astronaut is working without a tether. He is wearing a SAFER (Simplified Aid for EVA Rescue) backpack. It can be controlled by small jets of nitrogen, which allow the astronaut to fly back to the space station.

332 A safety tether stops astronauts from floating away from their spacecraft. It is like a rope with one end fixed to the spacecraft and the other to the spacesuit. Tools used by the astronauts are also tethered to the spacesuit so they don't get lost in space.

I DON'T BELIEVE IT!
Spacewalking astronauts may have to stay in their spacesuits for up to eight hours without a toilet break. They wear a Maximum Absorption Garment (MAG) under their spacesuit to absorb the waste.

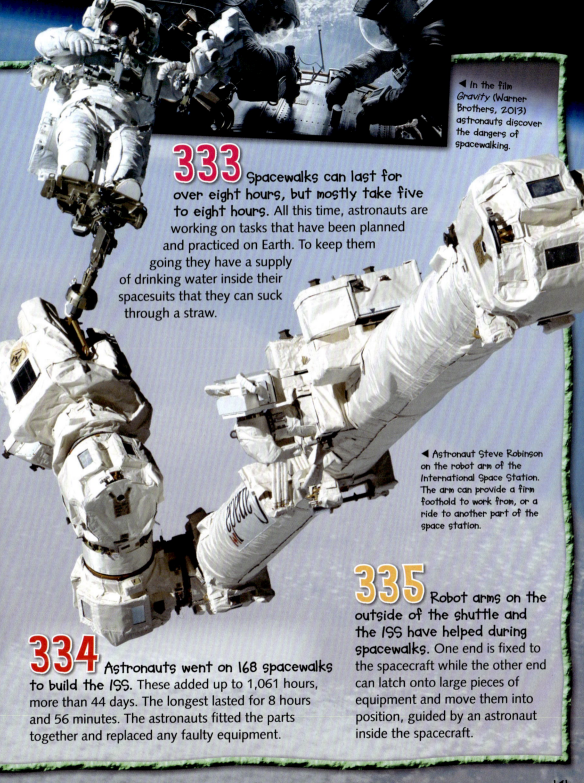

◀ In the film *Gravity* (Warner Brothers, 2013) astronauts discover the dangers of spacewalking.

333 Spacewalks can last for over eight hours, but mostly take five to eight hours. All this time, astronauts are working on tasks that have been planned and practiced on Earth. To keep them going they have a supply of drinking water inside their spacesuits that they can suck through a straw.

◀ Astronaut Steve Robinson on the robot arm of the International Space Station. The arm can provide a firm foothold to work from, or a ride to another part of the space station.

334 Astronauts went on 168 spacewalks to build the ISS. These added up to 1,061 hours, more than 44 days. The longest lasted for 8 hours and 56 minutes. The astronauts fitted the parts together and replaced any faulty equipment.

335 Robot arms on the outside of the shuttle and the ISS have helped during spacewalks. One end is fixed to the spacecraft while the other end can latch onto large pieces of equipment and move them into position, guided by an astronaut inside the spacecraft.

Living in space

336 **The first thing you would notice on a spaceflight is that everything floats.** This is called weightlessness. Spacecraft have footholds and straps to keep the astronauts in place while they are working or eating. Everything they use—notebooks, tools, cutlery, toiletries—must be fixed down or they would float away.

▼ Astronauts eating a meal from packets strapped to a table. They use spoons to eat the soft food.

I DON'T BELIEVE IT!
About half of all astronauts suffer from space sickness, rather like travel sickness on Earth. It makes them feel sick or confused, and some are actually sick. However, after a few days the feeling wears off as they get used to the weightlessness of space flight.

337 **All the food on the ISS is brought up from Earth.** A lot is dried to save weight, even the drinks. There is no refrigerator so the food is sealed in packets or cans to stop it going off. The astronauts add water to the packet and shake before eating. They drink through a straw from a closed pack because liquids would float out of an open cup.

▼❶ Wetting hair with drops of water.

▼❷ Rubbing shampoo through hair.

▲❸ Combing out clean hair.

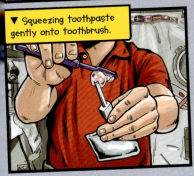
▼ Squeezing toothpaste gently onto toothbrush.

338 **The ISS has no shower.** Astronauts keep clean by washing with a soapy flannel. There is a limited supply of water because it must all be brought up from Earth, so they wash their hair with a special shampoo that doesn't need to be rinsed out. They also have edible toothpaste that they can swallow after brushing their teeth to avoid rinsing and spitting.

339 **When astronauts sleep they must strap themselves down so they don't float around and bump into things.** They usually sleep in sleeping bags fixed to a wall. There are small cabins in the ISS with just enough room for one astronaut in a sleeping bag. Some astronauts use sleep masks and earplugs to block out the noise and light.

▶ Many astronauts find it difficult to sleep soundly in space.

▼ Astronauts fasten themselves on to the toilet so they don't float off.

340 **You cannot flush a toilet with water in space.** Instead, air is used to suck the waste away from the astronauts' bodies. Urine is collected through a tube and cleaned, then the clean water is used again for drinking. All the water on the ISS is cleaned and recycled. The air is recirculated, removing the carbon dioxide breathed out by the astronauts and adding fresh oxygen.

Space stations

341 Astronauts live and work in space stations for months at a time while they are on a mission. The first space station to be launched was the Russian *Salyut 1* in 1971.

342 Modern space stations are built in space. The first one to be built in this way was called *Mir*. It took ten years, from 1986 to 1996, to assemble its six modules. The ISS is four times bigger, and took more than 115 space flights and over ten years to build.

343 The ISS is over 330 feet long, almost the length of a football field. The space occupied by the astronauts is as big as a five bedroomed house, and has two bathrooms and a gym. It weighs about 496 tons—as much as 320 cars. Six astronauts make up a full crew. There have been people living on board the ISS since November 2000.

▲ The U.S. Space Shuttle *Atlantis* docked with the Russian *Mir* space station in July 1995.

344 **The electricity to run the ISS comes from the Sun.** Eight huge pairs of solar panels, covered with solar cells, change sunlight into electricity. Each pair is about 115 feet long and 38 feet wide. Two panels end to end would stretch the width of a football field. Altogether they make the 75 to 90 kilowatts of power needed to keep the ISS running. The panels twist round to face the Sun so they can make more electricity.

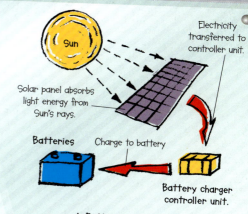

▲ Batteries provide power when the ISS is in the Earth's shadow.

345 **The basic structure of the ISS is a long beam called a truss that holds the parts together.** Attached to it are modules where the astronauts live and work, linked together by nodes. There are docking ports where visiting spacecraft lock on. This is also where supplies are unloaded and astronauts enter.

◀ The first module of the ISS was launched in 1998. Astronauts from 20 different countries have stayed in it since.

346 **The ISS orbits Earth every 90 minutes.** It can often be seen in a clear sky just before dawn or just after sunset. It looks like a bright star moving slowly across the sky. The website spotthestation.nasa.gov/sightings will tell you when and where to see it. Enter your country and city to find dates, times, which direction, and how high to look in the sky.

Space tourists

347 **A few very rich people have paid for a trip into space.** The first space tourist was an American called Dennis Tito, who flew to the International Space Station in a Soyuz spacecraft in 2001. His trip lasted for 8 days and cost $20 million.

▲ Cosmonaut Talgat Musabayev (right) helps Dennis Tito get used to weightlessness on his trip to the ISS.

348 Several private companies are now building space planes to take people on short flights into space. *SpaceShipTwo* is one space plane now making flights. It does not go into orbit, but takes six passengers into space for a short time before returning them to Earth.

▼ *SpaceShipTwo* is launched by a special aircraft called *White Knight Two*, which carries it to a height of 9.3 miles above Earth.

SPACE TRAVEL

▼ The cost of a stay in a future space hotel would be enormous—millions of dollars.

349 In the future, space hotels could be built in orbit. These would be similar to a space station, but for visiting tourists instead of working astronauts. One company called Bigelow Aerospace has already launched inflatable spacecraft that could be built into a hotel, but none that people could live in.

▼ A space station from the science fiction film *Elysium* (TriStar Pictures, 2013).

350 Other companies have suggested offering private space flights to land on the Moon, but one trip would cost billions of dollars. A cheaper option would be to fly in a huge loop around the Moon and back to Earth without landing. The passengers would get a close-up view of the Moon's surface, and would see the far side that cannot be seen from Earth.

I DON'T BELIEVE IT!
One space tourist has paid for two trips to the ISS. In 2007 Charles Simonyi spent 15 days in space, and enjoyed it so much he paid for a second visit in 2009, for another 14 days.

147

Exploring the Moon

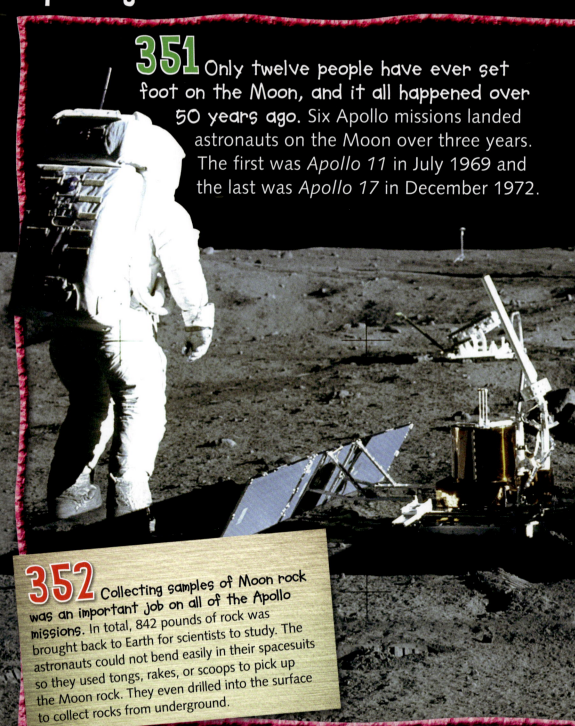

351 **Only twelve people have ever set foot on the Moon, and it all happened over 50 years ago.** Six Apollo missions landed astronauts on the Moon over three years. The first was *Apollo 11* in July 1969 and the last was *Apollo 17* in December 1972.

352 **Collecting samples of Moon rock was an important job on all of the Apollo missions.** In total, 842 pounds of rock was brought back to Earth for scientists to study. The astronauts could not bend easily in their spacesuits so they used tongs, rakes, or scoops to pick up the Moon rock. They even drilled into the surface to collect rocks from underground.

SPACE TRAVEL

▶ Buzz Aldrin sets up experiments near the Lunar Module during the *Apollo 11* mission.

353 On the Moon the astronauts had to wear very bulky spacesuits for protection. On Earth these were very heavy, weighing 180 pounds, similar to carrying another person around. But on the Moon the pull of gravity is much lower, and so they only weighed 31 pounds.

354 When the first astronauts returned to Earth from the Moon they had to stay in quarantine. They did not have contact with the outside world for three weeks in case they had brought back any dangerous bugs that could affect people on Earth.

355 Each of the Apollo missions left experiments on the Moon. These included a mirror, used to bounce a beam of laser light back to Earth to accurately measure the distance. Others listened for moon quakes and monitored radiation. All the information was sent back to Earth as radio signals. Some of the experiments still work today.

HOW MUCH WOULD YOU WEIGH ON THE MOON?

You will need:
a bathroom scale

Weigh yourself on the scale and make a note of your weight. Divide it by six. This is what you would weigh on the Moon. Find something that weighs this amount when you put it on the scale—that's how light you would feel on the Moon.

Satellites at work

356 As well as the ISS, hundreds of satellites constantly orbit Earth. Many are in an orbit called geostationary orbit, 22,236 miles above Earth. These circle at the same rate as Earth spins. This means that they stay above the same point on Earth, so aerials on the ground do not have to move to catch their signals.

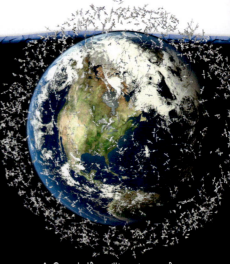

▲ Over half a million pieces of space junk also orbit Earth, making space travel even more dangerous.

Solar panels turn to face Sun.

Solar panels provide power.

◀ Aerials on Intelsat communications satellites relay radio signals from one part of the world to another.

Satellite points down to Earth.

Aerials send and receive radio signals.

357 Communications satellites send radio signals carrying telephone conversations and TV programs all around the world. Pictures of news and events from distant countries travel up to a satellite in space then back down to Earth to get to your TV. Satellites also let us talk on the phone to people thousands of miles away.

QUIZ

1. What kind of signals do communications satellites send?
2. How high above Earth is geostationary orbit?
3. Which kind of satellite watches cloud movements and measures temperatures?

Answers:
1. Radio signals 2. 22,236 miles 3. A meteorological or weather satellite

SPACE TRAVEL

358 Navigation satellites can tell you where you are, how fast you are moving, and direct you to where you are going. The Global Positioning System (GPS) has around 30 satellites circling Earth. Satnav equipment picks up signals from several satellites and uses the information to work out your position and speed.

▶ Each Navstar navigation satellite circles Earth twice every day, so that signals from at least four satellites are available everywhere on Earth.

359 Meteorological satellites help forecasters predict the weather. They look at Earth's atmosphere, watching cloud movements and measuring land and sea temperatures. The information is sent to huge computers, which use it to calculate weather forecasts.

▼ Solar and Heliospheric Observatory (SOHO) orbits between Earth and the Sun to give early warning of Sun storms.

360 Satellites looking down from space can spot pollution on Earth. They can also track wild animals and icebergs, and spot forest fires. Astronomical satellites look out into space to discover planets around distant stars, and find out what the Universe was like billions of years ago. Some watch the Sun for storms that could send dangerous bursts of radiation toward Earth.

Long distance space travel

361 A journey through space must be planned very carefully. Everything in space is moving very fast, so when launching a spacecraft mission planners have to decide which way to send it to make sure it doesn't miss its target.

▶ When *Voyager 2* flew by Jupiter in 1979 it used the giant planet's gravity to pick up speed and change direction for its rendezvous with Saturn.

Jupiter

Voyager 2

▲ *Voyager 2* captured close up pictures of the planet Neptune as it flew past in 1989.

362 Spacecraft can save fuel on a journey by swinging around a planet to gain speed. This is called a slingshot or gravity assist, because it uses the gravity of the planet to propel it on its way much faster. The Voyager 2 space probe flew past Jupiter, Saturn, Uranus, and Neptune to gain more speed to fly out of the Solar System.

I DON'T BELIEVE IT!

Launched in 1977, the *Voyager 1* space probe has now left the Solar System and is about 14.8 billion miles away. It is still sending back information, but its signals take around two days to reach Earth.

SPACE TRAVEL

363 Ion engines can provide extra speed over the vast distances in space. They use magnets to send a stream of tiny electrical particles called ions out of the engine, pushing the spacecraft forward. They only provide a very tiny thrust (push) but they can keep going, unlike rocket engines, which run out of fuel.

◀ The SMART-1 spacecraft used ion engines on its flight to the Moon in 2003.

364 Solar sails may also be used to push spacecraft along in the future. They are huge sheets of very thin, light material that are pushed along by sunlight. Spacecraft with solar sails would be launched by a rocket, then the sail would unfold. The sunlight gives a weak but constant push to the sail, which gradually gains speed. In 2010 Japan launched the first solar sailing spacecraft called IKAROS.

▼ In the future, huge solar sails like this could propel spacecraft through space.

365 Radio signals take a long time to travel to and from spacecraft far out in space. When controllers on Earth send instructions to a spacecraft exploring Mars, they may arrive up to 20 minutes later. This is much too late to stop a rover colliding with a rock, so many spacecraft are programmed to operate without instructions from Earth.

Robot travelers

366 Space probes are unmanned craft that travel through space to explore planets, moons, asteroids, and comets. Probes have investigated all the planets in our Solar System. They carry instruments and cameras to measure temperatures, radiation, and magnetism.

I DON'T BELIEVE IT!
Aerogel is an extremely light material, mostly made up of empty space. In 2004 the *Stardust* probe used aerogel to collect particles of comet dust as it could trap the tiny particles without damaging them.

▼ After a seven year journey to Saturn the *Cassini* probe dropped a smaller probe onto Saturn's moon Titan.

367 Some probes fly close to their target but do not stop. They collect pictures and information, then fly on. Others go into orbit around it. They can send back pictures of the whole surface and watch for changes. For a really close look, some spacecraft actually land on their target. They can find out what the surface is made of around their landing site.

SPACE TRAVEL

▼ The *Curiosity* rover moves very slowly, covering only about 100 feet in an hour.

368 The *Curiosity* rover is a robot spacecraft that is currently exploring the planet Mars. It is a six-wheeled rover about the size of a car that moves slowly across the dusty surface, steering to avoid any large rocks. It takes close-up pictures of the soil and rocks, and can drill into the rocks and test them to see what they are made of.

369 Several space probes have been sent out to intercept comets. *Giotto* was the first probe to send back pictures of a comet's nucleus, which cannot be seen from Earth. It photographed Halley's comet in 1986. The *Stardust* probe collected tiny dust particles from comet Wild 2's huge glowing tail in 2004. It flew back to Earth and delivered a capsule containing the samples, before continuing on to begin a new mission.

370 Asteroids (chunks of rock that orbit the Sun between the planets Mars and Jupiter) are also a target for space probes. *Hayabusa* is a Japanese probe that landed on a small asteroid called Itokawa in 2005. It brought a sample of asteroid dust back to Earth for scientists to study.

▶ *Giotto* flew into the tail of Halley's comet to get close-up pictures of the nucleus.

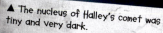

▲ The nucleus of Halley's comet was tiny and very dark.

A visit to Mars?

371 The next possible place for astronauts to visit is Mars. There have been plans to send people to Mars even before the first Moon landing, although it would be a very dangerous and expensive mission. People could not survive on Mars without spacesuits and they would need protection from radiation and the extreme cold.

▶ Astronauts on a visit to Mars could use a rover to explore Mars' rocky surface and as a base to live in.

Astronauts might not wear spacesuits inside the rover.

372 It would take six to nine months to travel to Mars, and the same for the trip back. One mission that has been suggested would fly two people to Mars, not to land, but to go around it and back to Earth. The trip would take nearly 17 months, and the crew would spend all of this time inside their spacecraft. If astronauts landed on Mars, they could be away from Earth for two years or more.

QUIZ

1. Is there water on Mars?
2. How long would a round trip to Mars take?
3. Could astronauts breathe the air on Mars?

Answers:
1. Yes, but it is frozen 2. 17 months if you did not stop and land on Mars 3. No, the air on Mars does not contain oxygen

SPACE TRAVEL

373 A mission to Mars would have to take supplies for the whole trip. There is some frozen water on Mars, which astronauts could use, but the air there does not have oxygen for them to breathe. There are also no plants or animals there to provide food.

374 A major problem during the journey through space and on Mars itself would be the dangerous radiation from the Sun. On Earth our atmosphere and magnetic field protects us from most of this radiation. Far out in space the astronauts would have to rely on their spacecraft for protection, but it would not protect them completely.

A Martian spacesuit would need to provide oxygen as well as protection from radiation and cold.

Astronauts check on the Martian weather and study the soil.

375 Having enough fuel for the journey back would also be a problem. At the end of the mission the spacecraft would need fuel to blast off from the surface of Mars and send it back to Earth. Scientists think that fuel could be produced on Mars using the carbon dioxide gas in the atmosphere. If so, they would only need to take fuel for the outward journey.

Index

Entries in **bold** refer to main subject entries. Entries in *italics* refer to illustrations

adaptive optics 64
Aldrin, Edwin "Buzz" 43, 90, 137, *137*, 149
amateur astronomy **80–81**
Andromeda galaxy 60
antennae 97, 99
Apollo 11 42
Apollo 15 43, *90–91*
Apollo missions 42, 43, *43*, **90–91**, 131, 137, **148–149**
Ariane 5 rockets 95, *126*, 127
Armstrong, Neil 42, 43, 90, 137, *137*
asteroid belt 23
asteroids 11, **22–23**, *23*, 45, **116–117**, *116–117*
astronauts 6, *6*, 15, **34–35**, *34*, 35, 36, *36*, 37, 42, *42*, 43, *43*, **134–135**
Atacama Desert 67
Atacama Large Millimeter Array (ALMA) 82
Atlantis space shuttle 33
Atlas rocket 125
atmospheres 9, *12*, 104
aurorae 20
Aztecs 51

Bayeux Tapestry 51, *51*
Beagle 2 lander 105, *105*
Big Bang 30, 31, *31*, **76**, **77**, *76–77*
binoculars 80
black holes 27, *27*, 41, **49**, 73, **83**
blue shift 69
booster rockets 32, *32*, 33
Braille (asteroid) 101
Bullet Cluster 29, *29*
Butterfly Nebula 48, *48*

Callisto 58, *78*
cameras 63, 80, 98, 107
Cassini-Huygens mission 8, 94, 97, *97*, 103, 104, 121
Cassini probe 154
Cassini spacecraft 79, *79*, 103, 121
Cassiopeia A 27, *27*
celestial sphere 53
Ceres 17, *17*, 116, 117
Chandra satellite 27
Chandra X-ray Observatory 71, *71*
Chandrayaan 1 spacecraft 91
China, ancient 50
Clementine spacecraft 91
Clervoy, Jean-Francois 134
clouds 12, 14, 15, 18, *18*, 19, 20, 21, 24, 25, 28, 40, *40*
Collins, Michael 43
Comet Borrelly 101

Comet Tempel 1 119
Comet Wild 2 119
comets 11, 22, **22–23**, *51*, **60**, **81**, *81*, 84, 85, **118–119**, *118–119*, 155, *155*
command modules 42, *42*, 43
communications satellites 40, *40*, 150, *150*
constellations **52–53**, 52, 53
Copernicus, Nicolaus 57, *57*
core, Earth's *12*, 12
Coronal Mass Ejection (CME) 74
Cosmic Background Radiation **76–77**, 77
cosmic microwave background 30
cosmonauts 36, 131, 134
Crab Nebula **70–71**
craters 13, 16, *16*, 23
crust, Earth's 12
Curiosity rover 111, *111*, 155, *155*
Cygnus X-1 27

dark matter 30
Dawn mission 117, *117*
Deep Impact spacecraft 105, *105*, 119
Deep Space 1 spacecraft 96, 101, *101*
Deep Space Network (DSN) 96, 97
Dione 103, *103*
dust 11, 15, 22, 24, 30, 34, 38
dwarf planets 17, 21, **61**

Eagle Nebula 60, *60*
Earth 6, *6*, 8, 9, *9*, 10, *10*, 11, **12–13**, 14, 15, 16, 18, 23, 26, 30, 32, 34, 37, *37*, 38, 40, *40–41*, 44, 45, 84, 112
eclipses 50
Egypt, ancient 50, 53, 55
elliptical galaxies 28, 29
Elysium (film) 147
Endurance robot submarine 93
engines 132, 153
Eris 17, *17*
escape velocity 94, *94*, 125
Europa 44, *44*, 58
European Extremely Large Telescope 83, *83*
European Space Agency (ESA) 87
exoplanets 45, *45*
Explorer 1 satellite 88
Extravehicular Activity (EVA) see spacewalking

Fermi Gamma-ray Space Telescope 71
flyby missions 92, 97, *97*, **100–101**, 120
food 142, *142*, 157
friction 131

Gagarin, Yuri 89, 136, *136*, 137
galaxies 6, **28–29**, *28*, *29*, 30, 31, **48–49**, *49*, **60**, **77**, *77*
Galilean moons *18*, 58, **58**
Galileo Galilei 18, **58**, *58*
Galileo space probe 39, **132–133**
Galileo spacecraft 39, 93, *93*, 120, *120*
gamma rays 70
Ganymede 58
gas 8, 9, 10, 11, 19, 20, 22, 24, 26, 27, *27*, 28, 30, 32, 38
gas giants **120–121**, *120*, *121*
Gemini North telescope 66, *66*
Genesis spacecraft 112, 113
geostationary orbit 150
Giotto probe 119, 155, *155*
gods 50, *50*, 51, *51*
GOES-18 satellite 83
Gran Telescopio Canarias 65, *65*
gravitational pulls 97
gravitometers 99
gravity 10, 24, 27, 32, **59**, **124–125**, 135, 149, 152
gravity assists (slingshots) 97, 152
Gravity (film) 141
Great Red Spot 18, *18*

Hale Bopp comet 81, *81*
Halley, Edmund 60
Halley's comet 22, 50, *51*, **60**, *60*, 119
Haumea 17
Hayabusa space probe 155
Hayabusa spacecraft 87, *87*, 117, *117*
heat shield 130
Helios 2 Sun probe 114, *114*
Herschel space telescope 71
Herschel, William 61, *61*
Hipparchus 53
Hopkins, Mike *122–123*
Hubble Space Telescope 19, **70**, *70*, **77**, **83**, *128*, 129

IKAROS spacecraft 153
impactors 105, *105*
infrared light 70, 71
Integral satellite 84, *84–85*
Integral telescope 71
International Space Station (ISS) **36–37**, *36–37*, 129, *129*, 137, 139, 141, *141*, 142, 143, **144–145**, *144–145*
Io 18, *58*
ion engines 153, *153*
ion thrusters 96, *96*
irregular galaxies 29
Irwin, Jim 43, *43*
Itokawa 87, 117, *117*

James Webb Space Telescope 83, *83*
Juno space probe 39, *39*

Jupiter 10–11, **18–19**, *18*, 20, 23, *23*, 38, 39, *39*, 44, 45, **56**, 58, *58*, **78**, 100, *100*, 120, *120*, 121

Keck telescopes 64, 65, 67, *67*
Kepler, Johannes 57, *57*
Kepler satellite 82, *82*
Kuiper Belt 17, *118*

lenses 58, 62
Leonid meteor shower 81, *81*
Leonov, Alexei 136, *136*, 137
light 68–69
light years 76, 125
living in space 135, **142–143**
landers 92, **104–105**, *104*, 108, 109
launch sites 86–87, *86–87*
launch windows 92
launching **94–95**, 95
Luna 1 and 2 spacecraft 88
Lunar Modules 42, 43, *43*, **149**
Lunar Reconnaissance Orbiter spacecraft 91
Lunar Rover 43, *43*
Lunar Roving Vehicle (LRV) 90
Lunokhod rovers 106, *106*

M81 galaxy 49, *49*
Magellan spacecraft 14, 79, 115
magnetic fields 113
magnetometers 99
magnitude 53
Makemake 17
manned spacecraft 133
mantle, Earth's *12*
Mariner 9 spacecraft 15, *15*
Mariner 10 spacecraft 115
Mars 10, 11, **14–15**, *15*, 23, 38, *38*, 39, 45, **56**, **79**, *84–85*, 96, 106, **110–111**, *110*
Mars Exploration Rovers (MERs) 39, *39*
Mars Express spacecraft 96, *96*, 111
Mars Global Surveyor spacecraft 102, *103*, 110
Mars missions 153, 155, **156–157**
Mars Pathfinder spacecraft 105, *105*, 111
Mars Reconnaissance Orbiter spacecraft 99, *99*, 111
Mars Science Laboratory rover 111, *111*
Mauna Kea Observatories 66, 67, *67*
Maximum Absorption Garment (MAG) 140
Mercury 10, 11, 14, **16–17**, *16*, 26, **56**, 84, 115
Messenger spacecraft 115, *115*
Messier, Charles 60
meteorological satellites 151

meteors 23, **81**, *81*
Milky Way Galaxy 26, 28, *28*, 29, **49**, *48–49*
Mir Space Station 137, 144, *144*
Miranda 20
mirrors 62, 63, *63*, 64, *65*
mission control centers 112–113
Moon buggies 90, *91*, 106, *106*
Moon, Earth's 9, *9*, 11, 13, *13*, 16, 17, **42–43**, *42*, *43*, 44, **54**, *54*, 62, *62*, 63, *84–85*, 88, 89, **90–91**
Moon missions 122, 137, *137*, **148–149**
moons 11, 18, *18*, 19, 20, *20*, 38, 39, 44, 45, *45*, 58, *78*, *79*

navigation satellites 151, *151*
NEA Eros 116
near-Earth asteroids (NEAs) 116
NEAR-Shoemaker spacecraft 116
nebulae 24, *24*, 25, 26, *26*, **48**, 60, *61*, 70, *70–71*
Neptune 11, **20–21**, *21*, 22, 38, **56**, **61**, **78**, *85*, 96, 100, *101*, 120, 121, *121*
New Horizons space probe 125
New Horizons spacecraft 17, *92–93*, 97
Newton, Isaac 59, *59*

Oberon 20
observatories **66–67**, *66*, *67*, 71
Olympus Mons 15
Oort cloud 118, *118*
orbiters **102–103**, *102*, *103*, 109, 128, *128*, 129, *129*, 144
orbits 17, 20, 21, *21*, 36, **57**, *57*, **59**, 124, *124*, 150
Orion Nebula 60, *60*

parachutes 33, *33*, 92, *92*, 104, *104*
Parker Solar Probe 114, 115
payloads 94
Pelican Nebula 47, *46–47*
Perseverance rover 111
Phoenix lander 87, 110, *111*
Pioneer 10 spacecraft 96
Pioneer 11 spacecraft 100, 121
Pioneer probes 45
Pioneer Venus spacecraft 115
planetary nebulae 26
planets 6, *6–7*, **10–11**, *10*, *11*, 12, *12*, 13, 14, *14*, 15, *15*, 16, *16*, 17, 18, *18*, 19, *19*, 20, *20*, 21, *21*, 23, 24, 26, 30, 38, *38*, 39, *39*, 45, *56–57*
Pluto **16–17**, *17*, 21, *21*, **61**
Pole Star 53

pollution 41
Polyakov, Valeri 137
probes 15, *15*, 17, 21, **38–39**, *39*, 45, **78**, **79**, *78–79*
Ptolemy 56, *56*

quarantine 149
Quintuplet cluster 48

radiation 70–71, 77
radio signals 40, 133, 149, 150, 153
radio telescopes **72–73**, *72–73*, 82
radio waves 70, 71, 72–73
red giant stars 26, *26*, 48
red shift 69
reentry **130–131**, *130*
reflecting telescopes 59, 62, *62*, 64–65, *64*, *65*
refracting telescopes 62, *62–63*
retro-thrusters 104
rings 19, *19*, 38, 45
Robinson, Steve *141*
robot arms 37, 108, *108*, 141, *141*
robot explorers **38–39**, *38*, *39*
robot spacecraft **154–155**
rocket engines 95, *95*, 126, 128
rockets **32–33**, *32*, 34, 39, 40, 42, 94
Rosetta spacecraft 116
Rosse Telescope 63, *63*
rovers **106–107**, *106*, 108, 109, 132, 149, 153, 155, *155*, *156*
Russia 36, 37

SAFER backpack *140*
Sakigake spacecraft 119
Salyut 1 space station 137, 144
satellite telescopes 41, *41*
satellites 27, 32, *32*, **40–41**, *40*, *41*, 124, 129, **150–151**
satnav satellites 151
Saturn 11, **18–19**, *19*, 20, 38, *42*, **56**, **65**, *65*, **78**, **79**, *79*, 100, 101, 103, 120, 121, *121*
Saturn V rockets 94, *94–95*
Shepard, Alan 137
shooting stars 81, *81*
Skylon 127
sleeping in space 143, *143*
SOHO spacecraft 75, 114
Solar and Heliospheric Observatory (SOHO) 151
Sojourner rover 111
solar eclipses 9, *9*, **50**
solar flares 8, 9
solar panels 36–37, 37, 132, 145, *145*, 150
solar prominences 8, 9
solar sails 153, *153*
Solar System **10–11**, *10*, *11*, 12, 17, 18, 20, 22, 45

solar wind 20, **74**
Soyuz spacecraft 127, 130, 131, *131*, 146
space hotels 147
space junk 150
space pioneers **136–137**
space planes 127, 146
space probes 132, 133, *132–133*, **154–155**
space shuttles 6, *32*, 33, *33*, 36, 127, **128–129**, *128*, 130, *130*, 131, 132, 137, 141, 144
space sickness 142
space stations 6, **36–37**, *36–37*, 137, **144–145**, 147
space telescopes **70–71**, *70–71*, 77, 83, 83
space tourists 37, **146–147**
Spacelab 129
spacesuits 6, 34, *34*, 43, **138–139**, *138–139*, 149, 156, *157*
spacewalking 129, 134, 135, 136, *136*, 139, **140–141**
spectrometers 103
speed 124, *124*, 125
spiral galaxies 29
Spirit and *Opportunity* space probes 79, *79*, 107, *107*, 111, *111*
Spitzer Space Telescope 71, *71*
Sputnik 1 satellite 88, *88*, 137
Square Kilometer Array radio telescope 82
Stardust probe 119, *119*, 154, 155
star clusters 25, *25*, 29
star maps **52**, **53**, *52–53*
stars 6, 8, 17, 23, **24–25**, *24–25*, **26–27**, 28, *28*, 29, 29, 30, 31, 38, 45, **48**, 68, 68, 69, 69
Stephan's Quintet 69
STEREO spacecraft 75, *75*, 102, *102*
Stonehenge 55, *54–55*
storms 15, *15*, 18, *18*, 21, 40
Suisei spacecraft 119
Sun **8–9**, *8*, *9*, 10, *10*, 11, 13, *13*, 14, 16, 17, 18, 20, 21, *21*, 23, 24, 25, 26, 28, 34, **50**, **74–75**, *74*, *75*, 84, *112*, **114–115**, *114*
sundials 55, *55*
sunspots 8, 9, **74**, *74*
supernovae 27, *27*, 48, 49
Surveyor 3 lander 89, *89*

telescopes 15, 19, 21, 27, 41, *41*, **58–59**, *59*, **60–61**, *61*, **62–63**, *63*, **64–65**, *64–65*, 66, 80, 82–83, *83*, 86, *86*
observatories **66–67**, *66*, *67*
radio **72–73**, *72*, *73*, 82
space **70–71**, *70*, 71, 83, *83*

Tereshkova, Valentina 136, *136*, 137
Thirty Meter Telescope 83
Titan 79, 103, *121*
Titan IV rockets 94
Titania 20
Tito, Dennis 37, 146, *146*
toilets in space 143, *143*
Tombaugh, Clyde 61
training 134, *134*
Transiting Exoplanet Survey Satellite 82
TV 40

UFOs 133
ultra-violet light 70
Ulysses Sun probe 114
Umbriel 20
Universe **30–31**, *30*, *31*, 41, 44, **49**, **76–77**, *76–77*
unmanned spacecraft 132, 154
Uranus 11, **20–21**, *20*, 38, **56**, **61**, 100, *101*, 120, 121, *121*
USA 33, 36, 37, 42

Van Allen Belts 88, *88*
Vega probes 119
Venera landers 104, *104*, 115
Venus 10, 11, **14–15**, *14*, 26, 56, 79, 80, *84*, 115, *115*
Venus Express spacecraft 115, *115*
Very Large Array (VLA) 73, *72–73*
Very Large Telescope (VLT) 67, *67*
Vesta 116, 117
Victoria Crater, Mars 98, *98*
Viking landers 38, *38*, 110, *110*
volcanoes 12, *14*, 15, 18
Vostok 1 spacecraft 89, *89*, 136
Voyager 1 space probes 152, *152*
Voyager 1 spacecraft 121
Voyager 2 21, 38, *38*, **78**, *78*, 100, *100–101*, 121

washing in space 143
water 12, 14, 34, 39, 44, *44*, 45, 141, 143, 157
weather 40
weather satellites 40, *40*, 151
weather stations 109, *109*
weightlessness 134, *134*, 142
white dwarf stars 26, *26*, **48**
winds 15, 18, 40

X-rays 27, 41, **70**, 71
X-ray telescopes 41
XMM Newton 71

Acknowledgments

The publishers would like to thank the following sources for the use of their photographs:
Key: t = top, b = bottom, l = left, r = right, c = center, bg = background

Front cover illustration Stuart Jackson Carter **Back cover** (l) European Space Agency/D. Ducros, (cl) NASA Images/ESA, and the Hubble Heritage (STScI/AURA)-ESA/Hubble Collaboration, (tr) NASA Images/NASA-JPL, (cr) NASA Images/NASA-HQ-GRIN
Endpapers NASA, ESA, and M. Livio and the Hubble 20th Anniversary Team (STScI)

Alamy 65(tl) Reuters; 107(tr) aberCPC

DepositPhotos 56(br) sergeyussr

Digital Vision 32(bl)

Dreamstime 5(bl) & 60(c) Kramer-1; 68(t) Silverstore

European Space Agency 96(cl) & 111(c) *Mars Express* D. Ducros

Fotolia.com 57(tl) Georgios Kollidas, (r) Konstantin Sutyagin; 60(tc) pdtnc; 60–61(bg) Jenny Solomon; 80(bl) Stephen Coburn, (c) Petar Ishmeriev, (cr) pelvidge, (b) Mats Tooming; 86(bl) Daniel Wagner

Getty 93(r) & 113(tr) & 132–133(c) Roger Ressmeyer/Corbis/VCG; 108–109(bg) Science & Society Picture Library; 109(br) J. R. Eyerman; 112(t) AFP; 120(b) Time Life Pictures; 125(m) Scott Andrews; 147(r) & 153(br) Victor Habbick Visions

iStockphoto.com 13(b) 101cats; 56–57(bg) Duncan Walker; 57(bl) & 58(cr) & 59(br) Steven Wynn; 60(tl) HultonArchive; 61(tc) Duncan Walker

NASA Images 5(tr) Great Images in NASA (NASA-GRIN); 8(tl), (bl), (bc); 9(cl) The Exploratorium; 13(tr), (br) JPL-Caltech; 14(tr) JPL/USGS, (b) JPL; 15(tr), (bl); 16(br) Johns Hopkins University Applied Physics Laboratory/Carnegie Institution of Washington; 18(br) JPL/University of Arizona, (bl), (br); 19(tr) JPL/Space Science Institute, (bl) E. Karkoschka (University of Arizona); 20(tl) ESA, and L. Lamy (Observatory of Paris, CNRS, CNES); 21(cl); 25(tr) ESA/STScI; 26(tr), (bl) ESA, K. Noll (STScI), (br) H. Richer (University of British Columbia); 27(tr) JPL-Caltech/STScI/CXC/SAO, (br) NASA/CXC; 29(tr), (tl) CXC/KIPAC/S.Allen et al; Radio: NRAO/VLA/G.Taylor; Infrared: NASA/ESA/McMaster Univ./W.Harris; (cl) ESA, and the Hubble Heritage (STScI/AURA)-ESA/Hubble Collaboration, (bl) ESA, A. Nota (ESA/STScI) et al, (br) ESA, M. Livio (STScI) and the Hubble Heritage Team (STScI/AURA); 30(bl) ESA, M. Postman (STScI), and the CLASH Team, (cr); 33(l), (m) Dick Clark; 34(tr); 35(b); 37(tr), 39(tr); 42(t); 43(m); 48(bl) Greatest Images in NASA (NASA-HQ-GRIN), (br) NASA Goddard Space Flight Center (NASA-GSFC); 49(tl) NASA Jet Propulsion Laboratory (NASA-JPL); 58(bl) NASA-JPL; 60(cl) NASA-HQ-GRIN, (bc) NASA-JPL, (br) NASA-JPL; 65(br) NASA-JPL; 70–71(c) NASA-JPL; 71(tr) NASA Marshall Space Flight Center (NASA-MSFC), (bl) NASA-JPL; 75(tl) NASA-JPL, (c) NASA-MSFC; 78(br) NASA-JPL; 79(cr) NASA-JPL, (br) NASA-JPL; 87(br) JPL-Caltech; 91(bl); 92(tl), (cr) JPL-Caltech; 92–93(c); 96(br) NASA-JPL; 98(c) JPL/University of Arizona; 100(c); 101(c), (tr), (tl), (br) NASA-JPL; 102–103(c) Stereo/NASA; 103(tl) NASA/JPL/Space Science Institute; 104–105(bc), (br); 108(bl) JPL-Caltech/Cornell; 110(bl) Goddard Space Flight Center Scientific Visualization Stud, (tl) *Mariner 4* JPL, (cr) *Mars 3* Russian Space Research Institute (IKI), (cr) *Viking Lander*, (br) *Sojourner* JPL-Caltech; 110–111(bg) JPL/Cornell; 111(tl) *Mars Global Surveyor*, (cr) *Spirit/Opportunity* rover JPL, (tr) *Reconnaissance Orbiter* JPL, (tr) JPL/UA/LOCKHEED MARTIN; 112–113(c), (bg); 113(br); 115(bl); 117(br); 119(cr), (br); 121(tl), (cr) JPL/Space Science Institute; 122–123(c); 124 (bg); 131(tr) Carla Cioffi; 134(tr) NASA-GRIN; 140(c) & 144(bl) NASA-GRIN; 146(t) NASA/Science Photo Library; 148–149(c) NASA-GRIN; 155(tl)

Reuters 87(tr) Kimimasa Mayama

Rex Features 63(cr) Nils Jorgensen; 105(tl) REX/Shutterstock; 136(tl) REX/Everett Collection, (tr); 146(b) REX/Shutterstock; 147(cl) REX/Snap Stills

Science Photo Library 17(c) Mark Garlick; 24–25(c) Mark Garlick; 46–47(c) J-P Metsavainio; 48–49(c) Chris Cook; 52(bl) Royal Astronomical Society; 53(tl) Detlev van Ravenswaay; 54(tr) Eckhard Slawik; 56(bc) Dr Jeremy Burgess; 56–57(c) NYPL/Science Source; 57(cl); 58–59(tc); 60(tr) Richard J. Wainscoat, Peter Arnold inc.; 62–63(c) J-P Metsavainio; 66(tr) David Nunuk; 67(tr) Adam Hart-Davis; 68–69(b) Christian Darkin; 69(tr) Dr Jean Lorre; 72–73(c) Peter Menzel; 73(br) NRAO/AUI/NSF; 75(br) NASA; 76–77(br) Mark Garlick; 77(tl) NASA/WMAP Science Team, (cr) NASA/ESA/STSCI/R.Williams, HDF-S Team; 80–81(bg) Frank Zullo; 81(tl) Detlev van Ravenswaay, (tr) Tony & Daphne Hallas; 82(r) NASA/Regina Mitchell-Ryall, Tom Farrar; 83(tr) European Space Agency, (cr) European Space Observatory; 84–85(c) European Space Agency, D. Ducros; 89(br) NASA; 95(c) David Ducros; 97(br) David Parker; 105(tr) NASA; 106(br) Detlev van Ravenswaay; 108–109(c) NASA/JPL-CALTECH; 111(b) NASA/JPL-CALTECH; 114(t) SOHO/ESA/NASA; 115(tl) NASA; 116(tl) Chris Butler; 119(t) NASA/JPL; 127(t) David Ducros, ESA; 129(br) NASA; 130(tr); 130–131(c) NASA; 134(c) Alexis Rosenfeld; 135(b) NASA; 141(c) NASA; 150(tr) Roger Harris, (c) David Ducros; 151(t) Friedrich Saurer, (br) Ton Kinsbergen; 152(c) Carlos Clarivan; 153(tl) David A. Hardy, FUTURES: 50 YEARS IN SPACE; 154(c) David Ducros; 155(b) David Parker, (br) EUROPEAN SPACE AGENCY; 156–157(c) Detlev van Ravenswaay

Shutterstock.com 2–3 Denis Tabler; 4–5(b) Karin Wassmer; 5(bg) Sura Nualpradid; 9(bl) Dimec; 12(bl) tororo reaction; 22(c) MarcelClemens; 23(b) Action Sports Photography; 28(c) John A Davis; 49(c) martiin/fluidworkshop; 50(cl) caesart; 51(c) Voropaev Vasiliy, (br) Gordon Galbraith; 54–55(c) ESB Essentials; 55(cr) Alex Hubenov; 60(tl frame) RDTMOR; 61(l) jordache; 63(bg) Vlue; 67(b) H.Damke; 75(tr) Dmitry Nikolajchuk; 86–87(c) pio3; 88–89(bg) Phase4Studios; 90–91(bg) Sura Nualpradid; 92–93(bg) nicholas belton/iStock/Getty; 96–97(bg) plavusa87; 97(c) jamie cross; 100–101(bg) plavusa87; 102(b) Shawn Hine; 118–119(c) Comet McNaught 2010/Primož Cigler/Shutterstock; 121(c) pall; 124(bl) J. Helgason, (panel, t) Rob Wilson, (panel, c) DenisKlimov, (br) Stephen Rees; 125(cr) caesart, (br) NRT; 127(cr) Shawn Hine; 128(bl), (bg) STILLFX; 129(tr) fluidworkshop; 144–145(m) Andrey Armyagov, (bg) R-studio; 145(t), (bg) Aleksandr Bryliaev; 146–147(bg) Procy; 148(bl) Jozef Sowa; 149(cr) cluckva, (bl) Baloncici; 152(bl); 154(br) nuttakit; 155(br), (bg) Petrov Stanislav; 156(bl) FotograFFF; 157(br) lukeruk

Topfoto.co.uk 141(t) United Archives

All other photographs are from: DigitalSTOCK, digitalvision, John Foxx, PhotoAlto, PhotoDisc, PhotoEssentials, PhotoPro, Stockbyte

All artworks are from the Miles Kelly Artwork Bank

Every effort has been made to acknowledge the source and copyright holder of each picture. Miles Kelly Publishing apologizes for any unintentional errors or omissions.